# Dramatic Personages

# Dramatic

## Denis de Rougemont

**Translated from the French by Richard Howard**

KENNIKAT PRESS
Port Washington, N. Y./London

# Personages

DRAMATIC PERSONAGES

Manufactured by Taylor Publishing Company     Dallas, Texas

ESSAY AND GENERAL LITERATURE INDEX REPRINT SERIES

# Introduction

Looking for a man and finding only an author, is the reader disappointed by the man or by the author? He is disappointed by the relation of one to the other; by the inadequate man who reveals himself in the author, hence by the author, too, who reveals too little of the man.

Usually an observation from the *Pensées* is quoted to establish a distinction between man and author to the latter's detriment. It is assumed that in general an author is worth less than a man; that he is, in a man, the share of artifices and deceptive appearances. But, in fact, nothing is less deceptive than a concerted appearance; nothing reveals so well the authentic man, that is, the combination of what he is and what he wants to be. The man without his work is not real, just as the work without its man remains a fine trap for psychologists. To separate them first in order to compare them better is to create the very type of the sophism, a problem of form and content, a problem of the chicken and the egg: Which of the two came first? Let us abide by the answer, quite Goethean in its humor, of the essayist Rudolf Kassner: "I leave the problem at the stage of the drama between the chicken and the egg, the subject and the object, and I shall not seek beyond the form—for there is no drama without form, and reciprocally."

How can we see a man's being outside of its manifestations? If, then, I concern myself with what is true in a man, it is in his work that I must seek it. For every work is the

v

testimony of a drama between the man and himself; it is this drama made visible; and it is in the drama that the total truth of a being resides. In this testimony of forms, to seek the man is to try to surprise the person. To see forms, to espouse rhythms—whether of language or of thought—is to perceive the momentary results and measure the degree of tension of the spiritual combat in which the man becomes the person and "authorizes himself" by a unique vocation.

Yet such visible and tangible testimonies remain for this very reason equivocal. And this results from the nature of the person revealed in them

If it is true that the pure person consists of the perfect coincidence of vocation and individual; and if our always-impure person consists of an approaching vocation which seizes upon an individual in order to orient his natural *données* toward goals revealed by the Spirit, it is evident that the person, pure or impure, will never be visible as such. For of the protagonists of this drama, only one falls within the apprehension of our senses: the natural individual. Even he is scarcely to be isolated from this work in which the "other" engages him. Ultimately, we see only the work, that is, the lists of the combat.

We would be certain of seeing the entire person in his acts only if we were certain of a perfect identity between the gestures of the individual and the summons of his vocation—and this vocation must still be *believed*. . . . We see, on the contrary, a struggle, resistances, and blows below the belt. All human persons are ambiguous, inadequate, and dramatic.

But then, is the absolute person merely a myth, a nostalgia, a presumptuous extrapolation, or just a translation of what Freud calls the "superego"? Has he ever existed in history? Has a man ever received the terrible gift of incarnating, without the slightest defect, the Word that was his true life, his vocation, his final goal?

Jesus Christ is that Man, which is why his historical reality, as it is attested by the Gospels, seems to us fundamentally inconceivable. And even the disciples, who saw him among them and touched him, could not believe in this Person. They saw and touched the individual Jesus, the carpenter of Nazareth. They also knew his vocation, announced by Scripture and designated by the name of Christ. But what neither "flesh nor blood" nor the reason which seeks to govern them, could believe and contemplate was the perfect identity of Jesus-Christ in one Person. For the man of flesh and reason, this hyphen will always remain inconceivable, this identity scandalous. Madness to the Greeks, says Saint Paul, and scandal to the Jews. One day Jesus asked his apostles: "Whom say ye that I am?" And Simon Peter answered: "Thou art the Christ, the Son of the living God." And Jesus answered, saying: "Blessed art thou, Simon Bar-jona: for flesh and blood hath not revealed *it* unto thee, but my Father which is in heaven" (Matt. XVI, 15–17).

Just as faith alone can acknowledge the vocation of the Christ incarnated in Jesus, faith alone can reveal to us our singular vocation when, acting by our hands, it personifies us in our turn. Thus our person remains hidden from us—remains "hidden with the Christ in God"—and it is only to the eyes of faith that certain of our acts appear to attest our obedience to the Eternal. Yet positivist analysis can always attribute these acts to purely human determinations. But if our person remains a mystery and a promise in our own eyes, what will it be in the eyes of others? And with what right do we claim to discern in a written work the testimony of a vocation which remains, in essence, incomparable?

Let us suppose the problem is solved. To know the unique greatness of a person is first of all to measure the singular tensions at the heart of which that person appears; it is to search the *données* of the individual who endures and accepts that person, to mime certain of his efforts in oneself, to enter into sympathy, by preference, perhaps, with what confounds us in his procedures. In a word, it is to love him. To re-invent his program. An impossible task, if the works of this man, and in particular his written works, did not come to the support of the undertaking. And that is why, in these studies of the person, I concern myself with writers. It is clear that they do not possess a particular privilege, but they have testified to their identity by certain specific documents whose charm and audacity guide me: I know the rules of this game, its difficulties are my own. I can therefore try some of their stratagems, the easiest among those which they suggest to me. Is this enough in order to judge them? Whether they have won or lost, they have gone farther than I shall ever go: It was *their* game, and their vital stake. How judge, then? How take these lives more seriously than they took themselves? Hence, I am cast back upon my uncertainty. . . . And yet this exercise of sympathy has made me more conscious of myself. I have *recognized,* here or there, in a turn of phrase, habit of thought, some moments of a secretly familiar drama. These forms, these formulas speak *me,* express *me.* They must have been born, under their author's hand, from a movement of faith or doubt analogous to those I experience.

Only Spirit recognizes Spirit, but certain material signs will always be necessary to us in order to fortify and nourish its intuitions. With their help, I can henceforth anticipate, in a work where they appear, the secret orientation, the inner coherence, the identity in the contradictions, which reveals the existence of the person.

It seems to me that any incarnation of a thought in a life or of a vocation in an individual "figures" the synthesis, in a single being, a single act, a single work, of two distinct or even contradictory natures, a form and a transforming agent, a resistance and an activity, whose conflict can be resolved only by the fact of a *creation.* The person knows himself in the acts by which he assumes, in unprecedented units which become accomplished facts, incompatible *données.* This way of comprehending and creating relations foreseen by no one else is precisely what we can call the "personal" style of an author, or in fact of any man responsible for his existence. It is a question of a phenomenon which transcends from the start the fact of writing and style in the narrow sense of the word. It is a question of a fundamental equation of the existent, whose elements it is the personalist critic's goal to seek in all elaborated *forms*—ethical, political, artistic . . .

Thus I have sought in the works of a Goethe, a Kierkegaard, or a Luther for the "personal" *données* whose reciprocal tension may have produced the *forms* we observe there. It is less the ideas that interest me than the drama instituted in a man by the gradual *information* of an idea, that is, its actualization. I believe that man has value only by what attacks him, provokes him to transcend himself and thereby manifest his true being, the intention of his existence.

Magic and Germanism overcome, ordered, and transvalued (in the Nietzschean sense of the word) by a will to action, whose victory is attested in *Faust*—that is what I call Goethe.

The opposition of the world's form and the mind which transforms it; the opposition of the solitary and the crowd, within the individual himself; the testimony of the demands of a faith, which seems incommensurable with life as organized by a Goethean wisdom—that is the content of a message which could find its completed form only in the unimpeachable fact of a martyrdom. Such was the vocation of Kierkegaard.

The anguish over a guilt which remains indecipherable to him, man's unendurable and too-lucid hesitation before the "absurdity" of the transcendant is the essentially enigmatic person of Franz Kafka; the negative, in a sense, of a vocation.

The triumph of a mortal and salutary word over a powerfully natural individual is the act authorizing Luther's doctrine.

These four figures, along with those of Calvin, Gide, and Lawrence, are disparate not only in their appearances. And their confrontation in these pages can be justified only as critical metaphors, thereby signifying the true subject of this work: "Man being given," as Claudel says, "to invent a common reason for terms infinitely distant and multiple."

"A man of wit," Kierkegaard says, "remarked that humanity could be divided into officers, chambermaids, and chimney sweeps. To me, this observation is not only witty, it is profound, and it takes a great speculative talent to afford a better division. When a classification does not exhaust its object ideally, *any other* is preferable to it at every point, because it has the advantage of setting the imagination in movement." That is the only advantage which I am reasonably entitled to expect from the publication of this group of studies.

And yet it seems to me, after the fact, that everything is not fortuitous in my collection.

Among the writers whose thought has transformed the data of our lives, I distinguish two great families. The first acts only by the objective content of its theories, not by its indifferent style. To it belong Hegel, Marx, or Sorel. On the other hand, a Pascal, a Kierkegaard, a Rimbaud act less by virtue of their conclusions than by that of their personal drama made "flesh" by the turns of their language, the movement of their thought. Only the authors of this second family have arrested me, to set me going again in my own direction. And this is one of the reasons for my choice. The other is that, like a Knight Templar, I have granted myself the right to hunt only leonine game.

Without forgetting, moreover, that according to Luther's phrase, we believe we hunt when it is often we who are hunted!

And this will be rather a kind of postface: I have not written criticism in this work but *spiritual exercises*. That they are difficult of access pertains to the law of the genre. That their tone is occasionally strained pertains to the nature of the subject I have embraced: the creative tension of the person. I offer the reader only an effort. I ask him to experience certain rhythms whose scope or energy propagate a power, an initiation to the drama in which it is now up to us to be the *personae. Incipit tragoedia!*

—D.d.R.

*August, 1939*

# Contents

# One

# Wisdom and Madness

**of the Person**

# 1 Goethe's Silence

"Man," Goethe says, "acknowledges and values only what he himself is in a position to do." Hence the misunderstanding which the example of Goethe's life always provokes. Those who find Goethe bourgeois merely betray a rationalism without tension, without grandeur; they do not see that the Faustian *sagesse* is primarily a defense against the Demon of revolt, against all latent Magic; indeed their failure to see this proves the success of the defense. On the other hand, they can easily see rebellion in those who parade it, and magic in those who vaticinate but fall short of Goethe in mastery of the mysteries—so they turn to Rimbaud.

Perhaps the confrontation of the Sage and the Madman, by the very vividness of the paradox, will afford a sharper and more effective awareness of the true Goethean powers.

The child Rimbaud writes "magical" poems, then renounces magic and falls silent. Goethe, an initiate in his youth, begins writing at about this period in his life, but once the fever abates, he continues his "literary activity" no less diligently. These two experiences would be antithetical if they could be superimposed, which of course is not the case. From the literary point of view, the confrontation is absurd, I allow. But is our perspective not distorted by a state of mind that would have us consider these two men chiefly as writers? It is by the written word that they are most antithetical. Yet Rimbaud was never a writer, and never concerned to be one. And Goethe was only a writer among other things. So it is not the literary aspect of these experiences that should condition our vision. Not that it is for a moment negligible, dealing as we are with two beings known primarily for their writings. But to account for them accurately, we must subordinate the literary aspect to the personal problem of these lives, to their equation of existence. And in one, as in the other, there is a revolution of the mind that entails both the refusal of magic and the passionate love of immediate effort.

What continually astonishes me is the resemblance of *form*—the essential, timeless similitude that appears in these two experiences when we abstract them from all the literature in which they enveloped their manifestations— a literature which has not lacked for additional volumes since. It should be noted, however, that such a confrontation would have exasperated Goethe as much perhaps as Rimbaud,[1] but, I think, in their individual *habitus* much more than in their common greatness. Only my belief in a universal analogy of the soul's profound reactions to its fate authorizes such a confrontation, and persuades me of its human interest. And if all this remains absurd in the eyes of those for whom the only thing that counts is a certain originality in the esthetic order—at best—I shall not be surprised. The point, here, is simply to render more

[1] Did Rimbaud read Goethe? In May 1873, he wrote from Roche to his friend E. Delahaye: "Soon I'll be sending you stamps so you can buy and send me Goethe's *Faust*, popular library edition. It costs a sou for shipping."

concrete, by the comparison of two lives that exemplified it in opposed styles, a human attitude which seems to be *common* to both.

That Goethe was familiar with "the judgment of great and secret things" (Jérôme Cardan) is so evident in all his works that we have no further need to solicit his biographers. Frequent reference has been made to the young Frankfort bourgeois' intimacy with the learned and fervent Fräulein von Klettenberg. But more than on an easily rarefied spirituality, the mysticism of the man who, as a boy, built an altar to Nature, fed on a renewed meditation of the Rosicrucians, and who even went as far as a few attempts at alchemy. Coquetry, critics have said—but there are no intermediary sentiments which do not in fact lead to plenitude for a mind like Goethe's. "We fear lest his fire will consume him," writes one of his friends of this period. "Goethe lives on a perpetual standing of war and psychical revolt." And he himself groans, with somber joy: "Miserable fate, which permits me nothing but extremes."

Jakob Böhme, Paracelsus, Swedenborg—the readings of his adolescence certainly represent one of those crises in his development in which the spiritual being discovers its true *form*. If, as in Goethe, it is a mystical form, that of the terrible "Die and become!"—and if he assumes it deliberately—it is an event which can normally be expressed only by a new quality of silence. Further, fate must concretely favor this inner assumption. By the instrument of what "chance" was it thus provoked in Goethe?

There is a fact of his youth whose importance, both historical and symbolic, cannot be exaggerated: Goethe's first contacts with mysticism immediately preceded a serious illness from which he was saved only by the intervention of a physician who described himself as an alchemist. Let us remember: In Goethe *on the threshold of initiation, there was not a revolt, there was a danger averted.* It was against what he henceforth called his Daîmon, against "the despotic oppression of the alarming elements that overwhelmed his soul," that he appealed to the arts of a disciplined magic. From the first, the question was raised for him in urgent and coercive terms: One must survive. Hence the seriousness with which he accepts the conditions of initiation, and the most difficult first of all, silence. Thus the first seductions of spiritual alienation, of all that is "strangest" in esoteric knowledge had no sooner touched the young Goethe than the body's weakness led him back to the concrete aspect of our condition. And it was only by undergoing a material application that magic, denying itself as speculation, could be integrated into the human equilibrium—a decisive incident which represents in miniature the whole dialectical drama of Goethe's life.

But this illness, and the convalescence from it, awakened in his mind the first creative temptations. Conceived under such auspices, it is only natural that literature later assumes for Goethe the quality of a spiritual discipline, an exercise, a concretely conditioned organic activity with limited objectives.

From this point on, Goethe's choice had found its form.

Now he would have to renew it perpetually during his whole life, and to understand, to experience to the point of suffering—which is "substance"—to what degree the renunciation of speculative magic is, in fact, merely a fulfillment of the true magic, the most difficult and the only one fruitful in human terms. For such a silence is not the absence of words. In Goethe it is an activity, one with a double effect. What could be more stirring, in a work stamped with the sign of maturity, than this radiant presence whose every underlying sentence we divine, and which nothing betrays so well as the very reserve of the expression. This is why we sense it more vividly in certain passages of the *Elective Affinities,* so translucent for all their apparent flatness, than in the *Tale of the Green Serpent,* too obviously esoteric. An equilibrium so hazardous that the long patience of genius alone was not enough to safeguard it. It required the discipline of suffering. At first, the verbal excesses of *Werther* drown out the inner voice, even noisily deny it. This is the act of a soul which still refuses suffering and shouts its refusal from the rooftops. A little more suffering, and more intimately secured, and then comes the other danger: ascetic delectation, the glacial obscurity of the *Mysteries.* A little more humility, in other words, the real desire to be "useful," and he reaches the perfect medium: the *Affinities.* The alternation of the three states, apparent throughout the whole of his work, proves moreover that the question is constantly raised anew, and, that for all the increasingly serene appearance, the temptation returns, the agony continues. Only the effort to create equilibrium has released new energies. Silence ripens under cover of secrecy, and in the deep, conceptions form. Thus magic, externally renounced for the sake of a "useful" expression, is reborn as though inwardly liberated to the "new day." The soul attains to that knowledge, that act of spiritual fecundation by which man penetrates mystical reality. And this act can occur only in the mind's *deepest silence,* in the region to which only the man who can preserve his passion at the core of an endless patience has access. Was it not this deepest strata that Jakob Böhme meant, that "contains the pure element, but also the dark being in the mystery of passion?"

This complex dialectic of magic was stylized by Goethe himself in the concrete symbols of his *Faust,* a work precisely coterminous with his own creative life, a work so autobiographical that he was tempted to incorporate the plan of certain acts into *Poetry and Truth.*

The drama opens with an awakening: The untrammeled exercise of the occult arts leaves Faust's mind gaping over the void: "I who believed myself greater than the Cherubim . . . who thought by creating to enjoy the life of the gods and make myself their equal . . . how much I must expiate!" Faust catches himself back from the brink of death. But for him, life will be no more than a profound renunciation; even if passion occupies him for a time, it is action—the great Goethean word—that will henceforth prevail. But it is an action which, in advance, despairs of the only success that is real for Faust: the happy possession of the moment. And when, exhausted but pacified, he is about to leave his blind body for other forms of existence which Nature is somehow constrained to assign to the *active*[2] man, we discover that it is magic, still, that has not ceased to shackle him:

*Könnt ich Magie von meinem Pfad entfernen*
*Die Zaubersprüche ganz und gar verlernen*
*Stünd ich, Natur! vor dir ein Mann allein,*
*Da wärs der Mühe wert, ein Mensch zu sein.*

(If I could drive Magic from my path,
Forget all its enchantments, then,
O Nature, I would stand before you as a man,
Then it would be worth the woe of being human.)

It is the whole secret drama of the work that is confessed in this exclamation: Each time Goethe invokes the, for him, sacred category of the human, everything is at stake.

But finally the Angels lift Faust above this agony symbolic of his whole existence, and it is their choir which one last time sings the law, at the very moment he is given the Grace to escape it:

*Wer immer strebend sich bemüht*
*Den können wir erlösen.*

(Who strives forever onward,
Him can we save.)

The great symbolic entities receive him in their harmony: This is the "Great Magic" which Faust at last recovers in the full possession of his forces and the assurance of his gaze. The soul, purified of its "old slough" by the blinding effort of life, enters the New Day and contemplates the Indescribable.

If *Faust* is the drama of a tremendous patience con-

[2] *Conversations with Eckermann*, February 4, 1829.

stantly tested, *A Season in Hell* is the drama of an avid
purity, and its fate is wagered on a single cast. Goethe's
greatness was to have been able to grow old; Rimbaud's
to have refused.

Shift the Faustian dialectic into the life of a young person, one still free of all social and cultural constraint—the
outlines will be simplified to a single schema, the rhythm
will accelerate to the point of explosion, the story will be
purified until it becomes myth. The initial datum is indeed
the same: the lure of a vision that transcends ordinary
life. Rimbaud flings himself upon it with all the passion
of a revolt that expresses primarily a fierce excess of vi-
tality rather than a physical suffering, and proceeds by a
rigorously logical movement to systematize his madness.
But the eruption of this "magic" is so violent that it certainly agonized the child; is it not to defend himself that
he speaks so loudly, that he boasts of his powers with a
strange exaggeration: "I became a fabulous opera." He
has pressed on through all the stages of initiation. But
one does not release such powers with impunity. "My
health was threatened. The terror came . . . I was ripe
for death. . . ." Then doubt appears, and with it conscience. "I see that my difficulties arise from my not having
realized soon enough that we are in the West." The West
is the mind incarnate. The incarnation involves "conditions." It is the vision of human labor, inexorable and revolting, yet how to escape it? Hallucination has collapsed,
giving way to a desolate stupor. "I can no longer speak.
Henceforth renunciation is fatal. I who called myself
magus or angel, free of all morality, I am brought down to

earth, with a duty to seek and harsh reality to embrace."
This is the cry of Faust himself!

*"One must be absolutely modern."* Work. Give oneself
up to the moment, to this hour that is "stern at the very
least." Earn forty thousand francs. Die obsessed by such
work.

Thus, this life is all of a piece; a single and unique experience fills it: the invasion of magic leading to renunciation and to action. The second Rimbaud is really the
same as the first, in a more "realized" phase. Modern man
is hardly suited to understand this, as he is hardly suited
for greatness and purity, and for commands like: "If thine
eye offend thee, pluck it out and cast it from thee." But
Rimbaud is of another temper; by writing the *Illuminations* he has already proved that he can violently renounce
one world of falsehood to create another. His life in Africa
is a second renunciation. The rest of us would have combined it all with a literary account of the adventure—for
it is not given to many men to become a myth by dint of
purity in the realization of their destiny.

Rimbaud is our Western myth, a Faustian myth. He
suffered tragically the Oriental temptation, condemned
and surpassed it, accepting like Goethe the real and given
conditions of his individual effort. The renunciation of the
evasive Orient is the very thing that constitutes our spiritual Occident. It is the refusal of "magic"[3] which is the

---

[3] By magic we mean here not only recourse to occult powers,
but also all our idealist, spiritualist, religious *evasions* (each of
these adjectives should be put in quotes, for all have been distorted).

basis of our ethic, and this dilemma is perhaps the most important the Western mind confronts once it has attained to those high-tension regions where any "orientation" it adopts is enough to determine a series of acts. A dilemma that is fundamentally religious, it is a dialectical, "agonic" form of the soul's life, a crucial form, i.e., one of those essential contradictions in the form of a cross that are the very sign of reality in Western consciousness. Remove one of the terms and life goes limp, the tragic evaporates. That this dialectical myth is profoundly constitutive of our being is suggested by the extension and diversity of its aspects. It is the opposition of knowledge and power, of wisdom and suffering, of speculation and existence, of mystical transcendence and ethical immediacy. And who are the greatest Occidentals? Those who have incarnated the boldest choice.

Pascal chose once and for all, in a lucid crisis, at the heart of a total passion. Rimbaud chose in an instinctive crisis that resembles the sudden collapse of drunkenness before a mortal danger looming up only a step away. Both achieve renunciation, the second phase of this dialectics, in a movement whose violence renders it unique; it is because they are both returning from a great distance, from a long capitulation to error. Goethe did not suffer such lacerations. It was he who was able to live this maxim from *A Season in Hell:* "No violent salvation games." From the first moments of his accession to the spiritual world, he put himself in a state of defense and deliberation. He advances thus, step by step, his soul disposed in a powerful circumspection, for sixty years, without ever abandoning himself to the blessed violences of the storm, to the repose of excess. Many laugh at his formal manners, the solemn banalities with which he gratifies poor Eckermann. In this behavior I can see only the sovereign distraction of a soul obsessed with mastering its gods. A lofty threat, invisible to everyone else, accompanies him ceaselessly; and it is from this threat that he draws his strength, ceaselessly renewed. But he must have a rare discretion, one so sustained that it gradually informs a kind of instinct, liberating the conscious mind. This is how the bold seer who wrote the mystical choruses of the second part of *Faust* can also figure as an official sage among the Philistines. The somnambulist is henceforth protected by a tunic of invisible silence. You can speak to him without disturbing him; words no longer reach his deep dream. And the Councilor's ceremonious attentions renew the old Germanic myth of the mantle that renders its wearer invisible.

This similitude of form in the course of magic for Goethe and Rimbaud, and on the other hand the contrast of rhythms, will be expressed in the resemblance of ethical conclusions and in the contrast of literary realizations.

*"My mind, take care! No violent salvation games. Train yourself."* An objurgation that might have come from some private diary of Goethe's from the ascetic years in Weimar, before Italy. And does not the famous passage from *A Season in Hell:* "*I who called myself magus or angel . . .*" strangely recall those lines from the first part

of *Faust* quoted above: "*I who believed myself greater than the Cherubim . . .*"

"*No hymns: hold the ground gained . . . the harsh reality to embrace . . .*" Of course the maxims of the old Olympian of the legend have little consonance with this pathetic creature. But what echo would *he* not have awakened in the soul of the young Councilor of thirty-two devoted at this period to the severest effort of organization of his inner silence, a period of withdrawal and refusal so painful that its sign became visible on his features. I never tire of musing on that passionately sad and dominating face as Klauer modeled it, the broad mouth with tight-pressed lips, the lower lip hollowed as though by a sob choked back, and loose at the corners—sadness and voluptuousness. But the forehead, of royal plenitude, juts strongly into light; and the eyes, between this mouth and this forehead, speak with a somber and meditative gaze the final word of the *Season,* that muted cry of lucid heroism: "*Et allons!*"

Only Goethe has gone to the point of conscious deliverance. There is in all despair both the anguish of the catastrophe and the secret, inadmissible joy of liberation. Impossible to isolate these two elements in Rimbaud's adventure. But in Goethe, it is the length of time itself which will reveal them. And that famous serenity of his old age is nothing more, perhaps, than the triumph of the liberating element of despair. The long pain of the man "who strives forever onward" has purified the body, and the soul is ready to receive "the love from on high." For such is the Occidental yoga for which the Second Part of *Faust* will remain a kind of sacred book.

That this liberating discipline involves for Rimbaud the abandonment of poetry—whereas it proposes writing to Goethe as a preferred exercise—is nothing but logical, and results from the very definition of such a yoga. Every *knowing* must be confirmed by a *doing,* which simultaneously conceals and expresses it. Rimbaud's *doing* cannot be literature, since for him writing means revealing the surreal and making the real miraculous. On the contrary, we might assert without too much paradox that Goethe's literature is one of the means of silence he commands, neither more nor less than the study of the natural sciences, the direction of a theater or the administration of a Grand Duchy. "I have always regarded my external activity and my production as purely symbolic, and ultimately it is quite indifferent to me whether I have made pots or plates."[4]

If nonetheless he took pains over the composition of *Iphigenia* or the *Ballades,* it was because for him art was the strongest temptation to play with the mysteries, and thereby the occasion constantly to realize afresh the last exigency of magic: its renunciation so that action may profit by it. Let us insist on this term profit; here, for once, it concerns the highest ends of earthly existence. "A fact of our life is not valuable because it is true, but because it means something[5] . . . It is very rare that we are ready to assimilate what is superior. That is why it is good, in ordinary life, to keep such things for oneself and to reveal only what is necessary in order for them to be of some

[4] *Conversations with Eckermann,* May 2, 1824.
[5] *Ibid.,* March 30, 1831.

advantage to others . . .[6] . . . Man is not born to solve the problem of the universe, but to seek where this problem leads, and then to maintain himself within the limits of the intelligible."[7] Here we discover the source of Goethe's strange refusal, in matters dealing with first causes and final ends, as such. Whence that agressive rationalism he opposes to the devout: "Concerning oneself with ideas relative to immortality," Goethe continued, "is suitable for men of the world and especially for the lovely ladies who have nothing else to do. But a superior man, who is already aware of being something here on earth, and who in consequence must every day work, fight, act, leaves the world-to-come in peace and is content with being active and useful in this one."[8] To which we might contrast this memorable avowal: "We may utter the highest maxims only insofar as they are useful to the world's well being. The others we should keep for ourselves; they will always be here to shed their luster over whatever we do, like the gentle light of a hidden sun."[9]

To write, and at the same time to keep silence. And only those will hear this silence who will have been able to perceive the taut, disciplined accents of the most even and serene pages of *Faust*.

Once this demoniac temperament is released from the role of a character committed to patience, we get eruptive confession: the *Illuminations* are the product of such an

[6] *Ibid.*, March 18, 1831.
[7] *Ibid.*, October 15, 1825.
[8] *Ibid.*, February 15, 1824.
[9] *Ibid.*, October 15, 1825.

explosion. They are the field[10] where Rimbaud gives himself up to spiritual experiment, where he yields himself entire. This is his purity; but it is also what ultimately forces him to evasion. The fury with which he forces himself to work "with his hands"—a frenzy of revenge—by its very excess is still an evasion of the real. In this he is a romantic, like all those whose violence or weakness precipitates them toward a transcendence of the conditions of living, beyond *this* time. But does our period have any further use for these evasions? It blames them on Christianity with more passion than justice, since it is precisely Christianity which asserts that eternity is in the moment: *Aeternitas non est temporis successio sine fine, sed nunc stans.*[11] It seeks this life. And all the rest, whether Marxist or Nietzschean, it calls other-worldly and rejects, thereby more Christian, more tragic than the romantic period— Nietzsche more Christian than his idea of Christianity, more Goethean as well.

But let us take care not to draw from this some criterion of judgment that would permit us to place Goethe "above" Rimbaud. It is Rimbaud's measureless purity which judges us, and Goethe's human greatness. And who would oppose them to each other? What would be the meaning of a choice whose operation would remain imaginary and vainglorious, so long as this purity and this greatness do not tempt our souls to the point of agony? Man can judge only *de haut en bas*. That is, he has no right to judgment

[10] And no longer symbolic.
[11] A scholastic formula by Schopenhauer in *Parerga and Paralipomena.*

here. Of course, there are points of appeal, of vision, other than human ones. The Christian revelation transcends our condition, if it fulfills it in other respects. This criterion of salvation, this transcendence, in good dialectics would authorize human judgments of value. But then we would have to balance a long fidelity—and perhaps a proud one as well, since Goethe regarded his weaknesses as errors not as sins—against a pride assumed and then renounced with the same violence, that violence of which it is written that it forces the gates of the Kingdom of Heaven. . . .

The fact that the times urge us to choose, even in our admirations, urge us to endow each thing, even spiritual things, with a kind of coefficient of utility. On this day of February, 1932, in this Frankfort at grips with the carnival and with anguish, it is not I who raise the question; the question besets me. The last carnival, perhaps, for this bourgeoisie[12] whose varnished treasures I have just admired in Goethe's high family home. Today . . .

Reality slips and bears us beyond the frame of a static and Cartesian logic into new regions of the mind, where action once again becomes our only criterion of coherence. Which is to say that we ask of the works we love that they bear witness to a certain power of revolt. Our first impulse takes us toward Rimbaud; we turn from Goethe. But let us take care not to fall into a reverse conformism, victims of sentimental values inherited from times past. Let us take care not to let ourselves be convinced by the mere luster of a truly splendid fanaticism. More than ever,

[12] The Hitlerian revolution took place in February, 1933 (*note from 1944*).

we must apply ourselves to distinguish in this intoxication the real power of a voice deliberately lowered. Goethe's silence is no less dangerous, for those who know how to listen to it, than Rimbaud's imprecation; and both constrain us to immediate tasks; that is: to the actualization of our reality. "One must be absolutely modern."

—*1932*

# 2 Goethe as Mediator

All greatnéss is produced by a relation, a tension between several *measurable* elements. No greatness is perceptible where no measurements exist. But where, in Goethe, are we to seek the elements of tension and the measurements? Where, if not in himself; I mean among what was given him and what he was able to make of these *données?* For in this Goethe is a modern man; his measurements are within himself and not in an external order which assigns him a place, a foreseeable and fitting career in a similarly well-ordered world. Ancient man fulfilled a function, and his fate was written in the stars; but modern man creates his destiny in the unknown.

Goethe is great by the relation, evident to us, of his life and his work, each according the other a meaning and a measurement. Perhaps we know no man's life so well in its organic, almost arborescent, development. Goethe's life, more than any other, is inseparable from his works; his works, at any given moment necessary and unforeseeable, re-establish a compromised equilibrium. Of no life does the law of development appear more harmonious and more powerful, to our eyes, through an incomparable wealth of foliage and adventitious growths. It is as if we were witnessing the tremendous spectacle of the growth of a giant oak. Here everything is organic; everything is *nature*. And Goethe knew it. But when we consider this venerable tree from a distance, its low branches sometimes strangely twisted, but rising so majestically toward its full development, toward that species of youth in the highest boughs, let us not forget that the substances, the elements which have made this splendor so eminently visible come from a Germanic soil.

To observe that the initial *données* in Goethe are German may seem an imbecility. Yet let us note the Nordic elements in the young Goethe's psychology: romanticism, love of magic, and that impulse which he will call *demoniac* and which weaves a tortuous figure through the whole of his secret life. Lastly, fed by these three sources, is the titanic will that is so magnificently expressed in the Prometheus. Had Goethe yielded to these inclinations which we might well call national, his work would incontestably deserve the adjective German. Yet, if it is true that Goethe followed his inclination, he proceeded, as Gide puts it, uphill.

From the fact that Goethe resisted the irreducible and irrational Germanic element which sought expression in him; from the fact that he suppressed demon, magic and titanism, that he became classical—are we to conclude that he is no longer German?

Let us distinguish between the results of the Goethean effort and that effort itself. It is easy to show what is not typically German in Goethe's written work, and what can be directly assimilable by a Latin temperament, for example. But the specific nature of the Goethean effort, that struggle against his anarchic and demoniac *données,* that struggle against something in him which was continually reborn throughout his life and threatened his dearly won equilibrium, that struggle, finally, in which his true tension and greatness abide—how can we fail to see that it is strictly German, even if, by its triumph, it leads Goethe to be *more* than German.

Facing the Goethe of twenty-six, the Goethe turning away from romanticism, let us set that Hölderlin who at the same age surrenders to the most awesome demonic powers, to the intoxication of the titans, to the vertigo of the heights: "One can fall into the heights as into the depths." We get an almost perfect antithesis. To Goethe, as to Hölderlin, opens, at this point in spiritual life, a career of excess and splendid madness. If he yields to it, Goethe will become not that tutelary oak (perhaps a little common) but one of those strange trees that shoot up in one season, produce a single flower, then die at once. But he prefers to prune a few branches, to subject to *his* law his powers; in other words, to educate them. He leaves for Weimar. He has chosen. He wants to endure; he wants to get well. And these are the ten years of silence and withdrawal, so moving and so pure, that is, so obedient to the deepest law of his nature. These are the ten years when, to return to our comparison, Goethe creates his trunk, his bark.

Confronting the titanism of Hölderlin—Hölderlin, or the German afflicted—Goethe represents the German mastered, the German cured. But cured by his own means, *more germanico,* one might say. For the very name of the cure to which he submits himself is difficult to translate into other languages.

Here we touch upon the national constant that is least questionable: language. It would be quite inadequate to say that the remedy Goethe administers to himself is action. If we wish to avoid all misunderstanding, we must resort, to characterize his therapeutics, to certain words that are eminently Goethean but almost untranslatable: the *Tätigkeit*, the *Tüchtigkeit* of *Hermann und Dorothea* and *Wilhelm Meister*, or the *Streben* of *Faust*.

To cure his irrational Germanism by the application of a Germanic remedy, and thereby to render usable and communicable what originally represented an irreducible value, such is the Goethean movement par excellence. But this formula risks remaining rather vague if we do not find an immediate concrete illustration for it. I see none more evident than the course of Magic in Goethe's life.

In the order of occult truths, Goethe first chooses the one that seems to him susceptible of vital application: magic.[1] This would be the place to recall the influences undergone before and after his twentieth year, those of Paracelsus, of Jakob Böhme, of Swedenborg. We know that with Fräulein von Klettenberg he even made experiments in alchemy, or, as he says in a letter of this period, in "cabalistic chemistry." I should like to emphasize, in particular, the fact that the serious illness from which he suffered at eighteen was cured by a Frankfort doctor who boasted he knew the remedies of the alchemists. Such is perhaps the *Erlebnis* which is the basis, for Goethe, of a

---

[1] Let us recall here the distinction—so important in the Renaissance—between magic and astrology. Astrology is the occult knowledge of the world's laws; magic is the science of action upon things.

conception of occultism that we might almost call pragmatic.

Besides, the problem of magic does not arise for Goethe as the technical problem of a science which would have to be explored more deeply. It is rather, for him, a moral problem: given the fact that magic exists, that there is a secret body of knowledge and occult means of acting upon things, what use have we the *right* to make of these truths? How can magic contribute to the organic development of the personality? This is the problem Faust raises in the celebrated first scene. Raises and even, in principle, solves in this scene. But for Goethe a solution of principle is never the real, existential solution. The whole of *Faust* will show that life alone, the *doing,* the *Streben,* can really settle the question, and not suppress the hero's occult knowledge; but on the contrary to internalize it, to instruct it in the microcosm of his own body, and then manifest it in acts, in activity, in effort.

Thus, Goethe, a modern man, first detaches magic from things on which, in principle, it was believed to function in the Middle Ages. For him it is no longer a trick effect, a device which functions in a quite external and impersonal way, but increasingly an internal, a moral experience. Goethe's magic is condensed into *speech,* into *Zaubersprüche,* which quite naturally and increasingly becomes in him precepts of action of a purely practical aspect; I would even say laboriously practical, recalling the annoyance which the constant preaching of *Tüchtigkeit* often provokes in the reader of *Wilhelm Meister.* Yet let us make no mistake. These precepts of such bourgeois appearance are first of all directed against Goethe himself, against his demonism; they constitute the cure for this single mortal malady to which Goethe reduces all other diseases, for this one illness which both nourishes the menace of magic and finds its antidote in a magic mastered. Thus, for Goethe, magic is a remedy from which he must free himself. No one ever coddled his sickness less than he. It is only when Faust, in the last scene of the human drama, blinded by his effort for redemption, dies in total renunciation that he is finally allowed to see, to contemplate, to rest in pure knowing. The Second Part of *Faust* is an anti-Goethe, or better still: It is Goethe's "person" triumphant over his "individual."

Such is Faust's wisdom: We have no need of revelations other than those which lead us to realize, in action, our personal law—a mediating wisdom, we might say; a wisdom which never mutilates, which never denies anything in the person that is irreducibly original; a wisdom whose masterful operation consists in making accessible to all lives, and to everyday life, the only real values which are, in origin, essential difference, incomparable secret.

Hence it is easy to see the reason for the cult that has been constituted around Goethe by the best German minds. In their eyes, Goethe represents the most harmonious resolution of the eminently Germanic dissonances. Nowhere more than in Germany can this particular greatness of Goethe be experienced with more gratitude; nowhere can it be so tonic.

But there is more. Because Goethe is a "German surmounted," if I may say so—and surmounted in the German fashion—because he was able to achieve in himself first the mediation between an irrational value and a general utility, he can offer us the model, the formula, and indeed the dynamic theme of a larger mediation: the mediation between the unique and irrational value of a nation on the one hand and the universal commonweal on the other.

There is no value except the personal and the original, that is, in the initial state, the incommunicable. The exaltation of such values in themselves, romantic nationalism, leads to war. The weakening of these values in their specificity, by the mindless multiplication of exchanges, leads to the internationalism of mediocrity. Only mediation, the effort to surmount one's idiosyncrasies in oneself first of all, in order to offer others only their highest and most useful results, can preserve both value and peace.

But mediation is the office of greatness alone. It is because Goethe is great—and we have just suggested the kind of greatness, national in its origin—that he is valid for us as well. It is because he is great that it has been possible for a certain German unity to express itself in his name, and not the converse. And it is, secondarily, because he has a national value that we can speak of his international value. If such an assertion were really only a truism in our time, the international problem that faces public opinion would be raised in a very different fashion. Peace by peoples is a snare, a formula of journalists. The office of modern peoples, insofar as they are conscious of themselves as distinct, seems indeed to be to hate one another. The office of elites is, on the contrary, to comprehend each other as distinct, that is, as *values*. Only, and from the first, elites comprehend each other. (Let them be recognized and judged by this qualification!) And it is in this sense especially that we must understand Goethe's great gnomic line:

*Über allen Gipfeln ist Ruh.*
(Upon all the peaks, there is peace.)

The elites, as such, meet in comprehension; whereas the masses, as masses, combat each other in confusion.[2] This is why our task—which Goethe would have approved—remains to federate *authentic differences,* and not to perpetuate washed-out mediocrities. The harmony of a painting results from the opposition of tones; it is a federal harmony.
—1932

[2] "National hatreds are vices of the populace," Goethe said. Nor am I overlooking this remark by a shrewd observer of political matters, William Martin: "The masses would gladly be internationalists; it is the elites that are nationalists." The observation seems to me true in this sense: that it is always the elites who have become aware of national values by traveling, by comparing. But it is clear that if these elites then adopt the passions of the masses (created by state propaganda), they betray their office of comprehension and cease to deserve the name of elites. Unfortunately, it is just this betrayal that is today baptized "nationalism."

# Kierkegaard

## Introduction

Søren Kierkegaard was born in Copenhagen in 1813, and died there in 1855. Almost the whole of his works, some twenty volumes, to which we may add eighteen volumes of posthumous papers, was composed in the space of twelve years.

Kierkegaard's father had spent his childhood tending sheep on the Jutland plain. One day, overcome by his poverty, he had climbed to the top of a hill and cursed the omnipotent God who was letting him die of hunger. This blasphemy darkened the rest of his life, and its subsequent disclosure to Søren was crucial in the son's religious development. But the challenge hurled to God seemed to bring the young shepherd luck. He became a tradesman and made his fortune. And it was in this fashion that Kierkegaard received as a legacy from his father, after a severe pietist education, a terrifying secret and economic security. From the secret he drew his work. His fortune he entrusted to one of his brothers, being reluctant to deal with the banks himself. When he died at the age of 42, almost nothing was left. This money was of a cursed provenance, he believed, and he therefore squandered it, chiefly in gifts. His own life was very simple. He worked most of the night. Georg Brandes reports that from the street Kierkegaard could be seen striding for hours through the lighted rooms of his apartment. In each room, he had placed a desk and paper, so that he could note down the sentences he composed as he walked. At dawn, he allowed himself some respite, strolled around the deserted docks of the harbor or walked out in the woods near the capital. Then he would go back to writing.

Around noon, he could be seen walking in the busiest street in town, talking, laughing, arguing with the merchants, girls, sweepers, intellectuals—with anyone. Everyone knew his figure, his jokes; he had his reputation as an "original." And everyone knew that he was the best writer in his country. His first work had an enormous success; but as he made himself better understood, the Danish public, alarmed, deserted him. When, in 1854, he began directly attacking, with extreme violence, official Christianity and the bishops who had praised his first works, he found himself abandoned to the most complete solitude a great mind has ever known. A year later, exhausted by the struggle, he collapsed during a walk through the city. He was taken to a hospital where he died calmly, "greeting all mankind." The only external event of his life was the breaking-off of his engagement to Regine Olsen. But the action which summarizes his entire work—that action after which, like Prince Hamlet, another Dane, he could die assured of having fulfilled his mission—was his attack against Christendom in the name of the Christ of the Gospels.

He had completed his theological studies, but he was never a pastor. Yet he occasionally preached; and his sermons, collected under the title of *Edifying Discourses*, fill several volumes. These were the only writings he published under his own name. All his esthetic and philosophical works, from *Repetition* to *Training in Christianity*, including the *Sickness unto Death* and *The Concept of Dread,* appeared under various symbolic pseudonyms. He meant this to signify that these works did not yet express the whole of his Christian message, and that he could not assume entire responsibility for them before God and men. It was only at the end of his life that he appeared unmasked in the struggle against the established Church, a struggle which was to lead him to death because it fulfilled his Christian vocation.

Kierkegaard has been compared to Nietzsche, to Dostoevski, to Pascal. He himself never sought comparisons with any but the great apostolic models: with Saint Paul, with Luther—but only to condemn himself. He declared that he was merely a poet with a "religious tendency" and not a "witness to the truth"; he had come to so pure and so absolute an idea of Christianity that he realized no man could ever call himself a Christian. This paradoxical position has made possible the most diverse interpretations. It also insures his thought a multiform influence, one that has increased with time. Contemporary German philosophy, with its two great masters, Heidegger and Jaspers, proceeds from his definition of "existence." Barth's theology derives from his principal thesis: the affirmation of an "infinite qualitative difference between God and man." The true and profound meaning of his entire work resides in his violent and humble protest, ironic and yet basically charitable, in favor of the evangelical absolute "Kierkegaard," as Rudolf Kassner says, "was the last great Protestant. He can only be compared to the founders of Christianity . . . All the others seem petty beside him. For Kierkegaard, the essential question was: how shall I become a Christian? Only a Protestant could find such a formula. . . . Kierkegaard's most profound and original work is his *Concept of Dread,* for which only Dostoevski offers an analogy. Kierkegaard, moreover, can only be placed beside the Russian poet. Both advance as equals, and no other mind of the century surpasses them."

No one today can measure the development promised to Kierkegaard's influence on our age, which rediscovers him after a century of obscurity. What is certain is that, unlike even a Nietzsche, no one will ever succeed in "using" Kierkegaard for political and temporal ends. He looms on the threshold of the period, the most radical denunciation of our collective cowardices, of our spiritual compromises, of our brief and restless passions.

On a Danish gravestone we may read this simple inscription: "The Solitary." Kierkegaard's laughter and stern passion, the powerful sneer and the message of ravaged love traverse our age like that stone and the word engraved upon it, which unceasingly accuse us in their eternal silence.


## Three Rhapsodies on Themes Borrowed from Søren Kierkegaard


### 1   Kierkegaard's purity

Most people live in an inconceivable confusion and feel no discomfort at doing so. Others, who try to think on Sundays, as they would do a little housecleaning in their apartment, soon retreat before the enormity—the absence of norm—of life as they find it. They go back to sleep, or else construct systems (which they will take care not to live in). Those who persist, however, realize that the enterprise might be fatally compromising. Thus the history of thought is often only the chronicle of its eloquent retreats. Very few follow their impulse to its end. One is accidental death, the other ruinous madness.

Only one man achieved in the intregrity of his strength a death which his entire work provoked and which, vanquished by such a victim, revealed to him in his last moments the true meaning, the value of destiny, of the thought that concluded there. To contemplate in his death the "end" of his passion and the fulfillment of his faith, such was Kierkegaard's fate, his immeasurable greatness. A matchless struggle to force the mind over the obstacle of despair and the absurdity of existence; a whole life strained toward the impossible, a whole work of exact sarcasm against the countless temptations of a religion which is not God—and, suddenly, on his deathbed, this ingenuously pietistic remark: "I do not mean that what I have said is evil. I have said it to get rid of evil, and so come to Halleluja! Halleluja! Halleluja!"[1]

Two documents illuminate the mystery of this life, truly "resolved" by this death. The first is by Kierkegaard:

[1] Halleluja: Praise the Eternal! —Kierkegaard has also noted, a few days previously: "For 1800 years of Christianity there has not been a task comparable to mine. In 'Christendom,' it appears for the first time. I know this, I also know what it has cost me, what I have suffered. I can express it only by the phrase: 'I was not as the others.' "

"To force men to take notice and to judge is the characteristic of genuine martyrdom. A true martyr never resorts to force, he strives with the help of impotence. He compels men to take note. God knows, they take notice—they kill him. But that is what he wants. He never believes that death could put a stop to his work, he understands that death is part of his work, indeed that his work only truly begins with his death!"[2]

We find the second document in the records of the hospital where Kierkegaard came to die. An intern transcribed the sick man's declarations: "He regards his sickness as fatal. His death would be necessary for the action to which he has devoted all his spiritual forces and his entire work as a writer . . . If he does not die, he says, he will continue his religious struggle, but he fears that it would then be weakened. On the contrary, his death will give strength to his attack and will, he believes, assure him victory."[3]

I   KIERKEGAARD IS DIFFICULT BECAUSE HE IS SIMPLE

He is despondent, but because of faith. And if he hopes, it is "by virtue of the absurd." He is not to be understood; he is to be suffered. He is loved, insulted, men dispute before his eyes, argue against his suffering, fear his corrosive pity. Finally, they yield and he refuses this capitulation. Kierkegaard is not studied; he is caught, like a disease. This man secretes a salutary poison, for which no one will find the antidote; that he died of it attests to this capital

[2] *The Point of View for My Work as an Author* (1848).
[3] Reported by Georg Brandes, in *Søren Kierkegaard, ein literariches Charakterbild.*

fact: the thought of faith can be irremediable. All the others, except Empedocles and Nietzsche, have refused to sign with their blood the pact which links the thinker to Mephisto or to Spirit—experimenters who reserve an escape hatch for themselves, warriors who lay down their arms before the fatal decision. Even when he renounces it, Pascal's reason is a concession; at its almost sadistic height, Dostoevski's pity is a concession. Yes, even these—even these two who advanced so far into the passion of the Christian absolute. Only Kierkegaard died of it.

An almost inhuman purity—that is what defines his greatness. A simplicity won at the expense of all that supports man against God. And yet, in this pure despair, never defiance, never *hubris*—purity of the Christian, not of the superman.

II  "PURITY OF HEART IS TO WILL ONE THING."[4]

I have heard the story of a young Frenchman who, out of disgust with a life he considers absurd, henceforth devotes all his time to chess. He has, nor wishes to have, no other interest. At least, such is the story, and I should like to believe it. I see nothing comical in the attitude of such a man—if in truth the figures of the game invaded his vision of life to the point where he could readily rediscover them in the most modest actions, such as eating, dressing, sleeping—for there must not, of course, remain the slightest place in such an existence for love, politics, etc. . . . With this proviso, we may praise this sage; he has been

[4] The theme of the religious discourse entitled *Purity of Heart*.

able to choose a thought sufficiently sterile and disabused by nature for its exercise to involve nothing "impure." If he has the strength to follow it to its conclusion, I mean to incarnate it to perfection, the issue cannot be in doubt. This thought leads him straight to a brilliant, symbolic *checkmate*. The superiority of such a man consists in this, that he has made himself capable of expressing his entire life at once. And his wisdom, perhaps, too, his secret irony, is precisely in having chosen to identify his being with a game, indeed, with that game in which chance plays no role, and in which final defeat is the result of severe reflection. This supposes a profoundly bitter view of the world; but at the same time an elegance, one might say a decorum in the grand style. This man must have purified himself of that repugnant kind of "seriousness" which attaches to certain of our contemporaries, that "seriousness" which causes them to be hailed as if they were someone, when they are precisely nothing but the scarcely comical prop of a respectable function, of a respected fortune. But for our maniac, nothing is serious if not the game, which is the concern of his life. And this is why his venture is worth thinking about. It might even define moral seriousness in the pure state: the faculty a man has of reducing his acts to the end he is pursuing with the greatest rigor. This said, it remains to be seen if his final failure will cast him into faith or into nothingness.

This is the moment to confess that I do not believe this story is as true as I have been assured, nor even perhaps as typical as I should like. Why? Because it is impossible that a man should never question himself as to the ultimate goal of his life. Yet this may seem to be the case for most people. Indeed, neither the low level of the answers nor the deceptions they often represent should jeopardize the existence of the question—especially in our man, whose ethical exigence does not appear mediocre. But if he has questioned himself, it is clear that his attitude henceforth implies something external to the rules of the chessboard alone. Relative to this implication, whose subversive nature[5] I suspect, the desire to devote oneself to chess is then no longer anything more than a challenge, a sarcasm, or, worse still, no more than an escape. The man does not stake his *all* on the foreseeable checkmate. He reserves a point of view concerning the game. That is his flaw, his secret discord. He will always have other games. There will always be an ambiguity. There cannot be a decisive purity.

A hundred other cases afford the same demonstration, but the latter is the least equivocal. Let us think of the great obsessives of history—Don Juan, Alexander and all the conquerors, Loyola and all the sectarians, Caligula and all the fanatics of unity, Nero who burned Rome to nourish his melancholy, Sade who believed in Reason, Robespierre who believed in Virtue, the great collectors, the great adventurers, and some dictators—all these "men of a single idea," all these profound maniacs—close as they have been to madness and to the total sovereignty of their idea, I say they have never known purity of heart, that purity which is to will one thing. They willed their idea, but also and always something else, something insignificant

---

[5] And which necessarily involves other increasingly complex relations, even re-introducing into this life, which we imagined so bare, all the confusion of the age.

perhaps, something no one would have dared compare to their idea, something just large enough to serve as a refuge, terrestrial or celestial, for *their* individual life, for their life against their idea, for their life despite their idea, for their private vision of that idea. Why? Because they knew that their idea could die—without them.

Love, the will to power, the passion for disaster, the sacrifice to an abstract divinity—so many principles of greatness and of reduction of chaos; but these are human principles, and thereby subject to human judgment. They can dominate an entire life and confer a great style upon it. But they always founder at the heart of man himself. They are powerless against his secret division. What I have done is not me. I am the difference that abides. I am the impurity of the universe I have created.

Purity of heart is to will one thing. To achieve it, must one cease to be oneself? The final failure of all human greatness is foreseeable once man flings himself toward a fate which he has chosen and which is the mask of his anxiety. But woe to the man who calculates and refuses to set out! The benefit of the experience is in the failure, not in the wisdom (here we approach the limits of a Goethe); but at least there must be that rashness without which a man would not even try to test his powers.

III   DIGRESSION ON PLAY AND THE SERIOUS

In general, play can be defined as a clearly *delimited* activity: it begins and ends at a given signal. But seriousness tinges it on all sides; the serious never ends; it is as long as life itself. And like real life, it does not involve any "repetition," any possible reprise of a failure. Still, the irrepressible effort of sin consists in refusing to acknowledge this seriousness that can only conclude in failure. We constantly try to "play" life, to reduce it to a system of reassuring conventions, to segment it into independent "matches." Even if we have just lost one, we can either start over or change the rules or cheat. And by a procedure habitual to the Serpent, it is these conventions, these invented rules, and this arbitrary segmenting that we now call "taking life seriously."

Therefore it is no longer possible to recognize and to separate play from the serious in our lives, to distinguish what is really personal from what is only mask or impersonation. A French writer, whose style is admired, declared recently that the Palace of Versailles lacks seriousness. This was well received. But in writing it, was our author serious, or was he merely phrase-making? What is serious is the only thing that remains important, but so many men pretend to be important, so many men "play" their seriousness; where is the difference?

*"Did the Apostle Paul have an official employment? —No, Paul had no official employment. —Did he have another way of earning a great deal of money? —No, he had no way of making money at all. —Was he at least married? —No, Paul wasn't married. —Well then, Paul wasn't a serious man? —No, Paul wasn't a serious man."* Here we have the dialectic of the serious and the ironic. It is by applying it to the apparently least "played" existence, that of the Christians, or of those who claimed to be Christians, that Kierkegaard finally achieves the only definition of the absolutely serious.

"*Official Christianity resembles the Christianity of the New Testament no more than the square resembles the circle. The teaching has become different . . .*" One is a Christian up to a certain point. . . . Yet "*every up-to-a-certain point is theatrical, it is a purchase on the abyss, an illusion. Only the all-or-nothing truly grasps the absolute.*" The situation of those who are Christians only on Sunday, or in a certain delimited sector of their lives, in a certain "measure" compatible with social life, is the situation of play, not of the serious. "*It resembles the situation of the New Testament no more than a petit-bourgeois salon resembles the most terrible decisions of the cruellest reality.*" And again: "*Christianity has been relegated to a finite commensurabilty. Under these conditions, men suppose they can take it with them without paying too dearly for it.*"

A religion which is referred to time and which seeks to triumph within time is not serious; it is limited. Kierkegaard casts discredit upon it by the irony of eternity.

For, indeed, eternity is an irony upon time, an irony under whose gaze time will soon succumb: at our death, at the last judgment. Having annihilated in himself all vanities other than the very one of hating time—this is his *lover's quarrel*—Kierkegaard can at last speak with that infinite seriousness whose meaning only Nietzsche, in our period, seems to have retained. Yet the philosopher of the Eternal Return possesses only a tragic nostalgia for it. For the "return of time" is ultimately a last flight before eternity. The substance of true seriousness can exist only in the act that makes eternity present. The mere *fait accompli* of the act of faith casts over all our postures and playthings a suspicion of irony infinitely graver than irony itself. For perhaps the act of faith does not exist, is only a figure of pious rhetoric, an illusion, a myth, a leap into the abyss. . . . And then there is no true seriousness anywhere. But perhaps, too, this act does exist somewhere, and then there is no seriousness in my life so long as I have not found faith, or better still, so long as faith, which is the gift of God, has not found and conquered me. . . .

To have known this is to "will one thing."

## IV  ONE MUST HAVE REACHED THE HEART OF THE MATTER IN ORDER TO LIVE IN SIMPLE CATEGORIES

But what does it mean, to reach the heart of the matter? It is to touch the limits of our condition and of the ideals which that condition invents; and it is also to acknowledge all our powers of chaos. True, there is greatness only in a simple life, but a life has nothing truly simple about it unless a decision has reduced it to simplicity, which is never native, never naïve. For we are born in sin, that is, in the inextricable. So that each demand that appears in us reveals a new complex. And simplicity never results except from a *refusal* to accept our *données* and our potentialities.

Greatness enters a life only from without. This means that it is not in the dimensions of events, but only in the simplicity of the singular and intimate relations which institute a personal tension.

But then, how can the man who reveals himself as multitude and plebs, on his own authority, impose any silence other than the silence of death upon himself? Here reason is commonly invoked. It is readily delegated this function, because reason is known to be powerless against the fundamental passions. It condemns them for form's sake: it frames solemn laws; and it is one of life's pleasures to contravene them. We create in serenity or suffering (depending on our tastes) a harmony, proportions, greatness, perhaps even an heroic ethic. But we know what all this consists of. We know what the threat is worth.

Only one reality can come from without and threaten all human order and disorder with crucial seriousness. Only one reality can threaten us with greatness. And that is the faith *"which does not come from ourselves."*

*"So long as I live, I live in contradiction, for life itself is a contradiction. On the one hand, there is eternal truth, and on the other, the diversity of existence, which man as such cannot penetrate. He would have to be omniscient. Thus the only link is faith."* (*Journal*)

### v "Archimedes' Point Outside the World Is a High Room Where Man Prays in Rectitude"[6]

A solitary before God. Then everything comes down to a single relation, the very one which establishes the human person. No other principle of unity *exists,* in the active sense in which Kierkegaard uses this word.

If we do not believe in God, that is, if we do not

[6] *Life and Kingdom of Love.*

believe that God is the original and ultimate form of *thou*, we will consider Kierkegaard the pure anarchist, the insane individual, isolated man. But man is no longer alone precisely when he reaches the very depths of the abyss of his solitude. For there he finds himself in the presence of God Who made him from nothing, but Who made him. Alone before himself, he would doubt his existence. Alone before God, he sees himself condemned, questioned, obliged to answer, and incapable of answering other than the "Thou Who art omnipotent" which immediately becomes: "By Thee, I can do what Thou wouldst have me do." This is the point of the greatest simplicity. But also of the greatest paradox. For simplicity is not such poverty as is supposed, that Cartesian clarity, that two-and-two-make-four, to which faith replies that one and one make all. This is what we seek to understand, but what we can only live, and what further supposes that man has first of all accepted being nothing!

The man who dies before God, as an individual, is reborn at the same moment as a vocation. This resolves nothing, or rather it resolves all our contradictions in the single *risk* of a dignity or an indignity whose measure is not of this world, though everything is ventured in this world.

## VI   FAITH IS NOT A SOLUTION BUT THE FORMULATION OF OUR PROBLEMS

Simply because it introduces into our lives the immeasurable requirement of the act; or, again, because that supreme degree of consonance with ourselves, which is the result of our vocation, corresponds to the supreme discord with our life in the world. Then what is faith? An immeasurable exaggeration? Obviously, for the man who has no faith. But the man in the grip of faith no longer measures his act. This is because he is no longer separate from this act. He is nothing *other* than this act, not existing outside his vocation. What would he fear, since he no longer sees himself? He advances in his freedom, and no longer knows anything of what measures us.

This man who advances into the world, against the world which will be saved only with regard to the solitary, this man no longer belongs to the form of the world but only to its transformation.

*"The world is an extremely confused thinker who by the abundance of his ideas no longer finds the time or the patience to think one idea."*[7] But the believer knows that *"imperial voluptuousness of never leaving the ways of one thought, and of never being frightened by it."*[8] And how could he be afraid of the idea, since he *is* that idea and that order of God? Since he no longer fears himself? Since his death is behind him.

Only one man, then, can be heroic: the man faith leads into immediate purity. All the rest is only defiance, intemperance, and despair. *"To dare be truly oneself, to dare realize an individual, not such and so, but this one, isolated before God, alone in the immensity of his effort*

[7] *Life and Kingdom of Love.*
[8] *Either/Or.*

*and his responsibility: that is Christian heroism . . ."*
Kierkegaard also adds: *". . . and let us admit, its probable
rarity."* For all this leads to martyrdom, as the churches
know. They tend to insist on something else. It seems
they prefer to *keep* their faithful . . . But the question
rises: who then are the faithful?

To the expostulation: "We cannot all be martyrs!"
Kierkegaard replies: "Would it not be better if each
of us said for himself: I cannot. If it is madness for all to
believe they must be martyrs; it is also madness for none
to desire martyrdom."

## VII

*Sancta simplicitas!* pronounces the martyr Jan Hus,
when from the height of his pyre he sees an old woman,
bent double by her burden, bringing her faggot too—
piously.

But the simplicity is sacred only in Jan Hus at that
moment. The old woman's is innocence, natural and
apprehensive religion. It belongs to the form of the
world, but martyrdom to its Judge alone.

## 2  The Act According to Kierkegaard

"All my activity as an author," Kierkegaard tells us,
"relates to this one problem: how to become a Christian."
For one is not *born* a Christian, and even in a strict
sense, one cannot *be* a Christian, but one must unceas-

ingly become a Christian. And the problem then becomes the problem of the act.

Are there acts? Man today does not believe in them. He believes in laws, and in himself as determined. Yet he is determined precisely to the degree that he accepts being determined; but to this very degree he ceases being human. For man has a strictly human existence only when he participates in the transformation of the world. In other words, he is animal and subject to the form of things—to the common degradation.

Those who do not believe in the act no longer know the way. How advance if there is no way? they say in their self-sufficiency—for this is what their anxiety is called.

In truth, all the learned demonstrations that have been made for a century to prove that the act is impossible and that man's totality is subject to calculation, the entire effort of the sciences and sociologies establishes at great cost the evidence of despair: modern man has lost his "way."

*I am the way, the truth, and the life,* Christ says.

## I   TRUTH IS THE WAY

*"Christ is the Truth in this sense, that to be the truth is the only true explication of the truth . . . To be the truth is to know the truth, and Christ would never have known the truth had he not been the truth; and no man knows more of the truth than what he incarnates of it."*[9]

This then is the mystery: If there is no way, we cannot

[9] *Training in Christianity.*

advance; but if we do not advance, there is no way. Only faith in Christ permits us to break out of this magic circle in which the demon's argument confines us—the serpent biting its tail. Faith in Christ is the necessary and sufficient condition of every true act, of every advance, creation, and victory over necessity.

"I am the way." But a way is a way only if we advance upon it.[10] If not, it is only a point of view, or else the site of a pure possibility; and here despair reigns. Hence, we must act, if we desire the truth; act in truth, that is, act in Christ.

Hence, there is no act possible, no true and living act outside of faith in Christ. But to believe in Christ is to believe in the paradox of the incarnation; it is to believe that God has assumed the form of this world; it is to believe that this form can be transformed. Of course, we can act "only by virtue of the absurd"; but this alone gives meaning to our lives.

Then the rules, the moralities, and the laws that told us to act, even as they deprived us of all power to act, disappear and die in the pages of books. At the first step we take in our darkness the way is illuminated and the prospects clear. And now we shall know that only the act of faith is creation, transformation, pure novelty in

[10] In this sense the category recently "discovered" by our psychologists of what "is done in the doing" is a Christian antilogy in the first place, rather than Hindu. For the Hindu, it is still only a form of human agitation. For the Christian, it signifies an effective transformation. Or better still, for the Hindu, this category supposes the primacy of a Spirit without content; for the Christian, the primacy of a Person.

the world, vocation and person attested, prophecy of
the eternity proceeding toward us.

II   ALL ACTION IS PROPHETIC ACTION

What is to prophesy, if not to speak the Word that
determines our future? But the Word is spoken only in
faith; faith exists only in the act; and this act then becomes our way and our law.

Thus we can know only what we prophesy.

The Christian advances in darkness creating his light
and his path,[11] a light which is not *his* light, a path
which evades doubt and pride, but which prophecy sometimes causes to gleam before him like a flash of lightning.
"Know that in the beginning," Kassner says, "all creation,
the sun, the earth, the moon, plants, animals and stones,
all spoke and prophesied, even as the prophets. It is from
this beginning that each thing draws its strength and its
time; every creature languishes after this beginning,
and fortunate is he who in his end possesses his beginning.[12] But man, fallen from his eternal origin, has lost
the vision of his end. Hence, he is a prisoner of forms and
numbers, subject to the laws of a world over which he
should rule. Only the prophetic Word that reaches him
like a call in the darkness can deliver him. Some receive
the order to speak, and that is their action, their prophecy,
and their salvation—even as men strike them upon the
mouth. Kierkegaard was among those believers whose

11 "Thy word *is* a lamp unto my feet, and a light unto my path,"
says the Psalmist.
12 *Die Chimäre.*

prophetic vocation, like that of the Men of God under the Old Covenant, is identified with the word that will lead them to martyrdom. The Word spoken is their way, their truth, and their life in this world; they die of having spoken it, and have no other task.[13]

The way is unforeseeable; ours, we say, is not that of the prophets. Yet the question abides: How act and how transform—that is, how obey the Word that prophesies?

The way is unforeseeable. What we know, however, is its point of departure. The way begins with every man who takes it as his duty to obey the order he receives from God—any and every man, at whatever order received and without any preparation.

How does a man become a Christian? *"Quite simply: take any rule of Christian action—dare put it in practice. The action which you will thus introduce into reality will bear the mark of the absolute: it is the mark of all that is truly Christian."* (*Journal*)

Sell your possessions and give the money to the poor, for instance, or if you have no possessions, cease coveting them and live like a Christian: from day to day, without assurances and without preparation, by the grace of God, in confidence and anxiety—one might say in a kind of *humor*—in the adventure of a man whom nothing protects and the prudence of a man who listens, in the torment and the joy of a daily discovery of the way; your

---

[13] "The prophet rises and falls with his mission." (Karl Barth) He has no biography. Nothing would be more ridiculous than to try to analyze the psychology of a prophet, or else it would then be reduced to the syntax and the style of his message.

way, on which you are alone, for it is the word of your
life, its measure and its vocation, its risk visible at every
moment, and its security hidden at the heart of risk.

III  WE ARE NOT TO FOLLOW THE WAY, BUT TO IN-
VENT IT AT EVERY STEP

As long as we consider Christ with the eyes of a
moralist, as a moral personality of ultimate significance
whom we need merely imitate, the act remains a pure
possibility, a model of an act, an abstraction—that is,
something that we can conceive without thereby transforming ourselves, and that is indeed the definition of the
"inactual." To conform to this pious ideal is not only
not acting, is not only limiting the role of faith in advance, that is, refusing faith; it is perhaps simply to ape
a flattering and reassuring model. And why? *Because
the way is invisible so long as we are not advancing upon
it.* Because it is a blasphemy of the pious man, of the
moralist, to claim to imitate the model his eyes see and
his flesh perceives (in reading the Gospel, for instance),
instead of listening to the order, instead of believing and
taking a step in the darkness upon that "way" which is
the present Christ.

There are abysses between these two demands: the
abyss between human merits and grace, the abyss between imitation and act, the abyss between religion and
faith, between time and the creating moment, between
form and transformation: *"One must not begin by imitation, but by grace. The imitation will follow as a fruit of
the recognition . . . Everything begins with the joy of*

*being loved—and afterwards comes the effort to please,
constantly exalted by the certainty that one is loved
now, and even if the effort fails."*[14]

Because one is loved now, to advance now, by faith,
upon that way which begins at one's feet—that is the Christian's destiny. It is his "impossible" destiny, the only act
possible for man. And it is the act which God initiates.

IV   "IN RELATION TO THE ABSOLUTE, ONLY THE PRESENT TENSE EXISTS"[15]

We know nothing of Christ, of the "way," outside the
act of faith which, supressing all historical distance, makes
us contemporaries of his incarnation. Thus the act of
faith destroys the time in which it takes place, but at fulfillment destroys relativity. The act of faith is this
inconceivable contact of eternity with our duration, and
we can say nothing of it except that it has happened and
that it may happen without anything preparing us for it.
"For God can do anything, at any moment. That is the
sanctity of faith."[16]

If we lived in obedience and in faith, there would be
neither past nor future, but the eternal Day of presence
in God and self would prevail over the world and the
whole of the human race. If we lived in obedience and
in faith, history would stop like the breathing of a man
struck by beauty, and motionless time would be engulfed

[14] *Journal:* "The imitation will follow"; in German: *die Nachfolge wird nachfolgen.*
[15] *Training in Christianity.*
[16] *The Sickness unto Death.*

in the eternal *amen. Aeternitas non est temporis successio sine fine, sed nunc stans.* Eternity has walked upon earth: thus Christ is the way. But we have refused the eternal and to it prefer our lives; that is why we are living in history, and in absence, or in nostalgia for the time to come; that is why we have no further being save by faith, "substance of things hoped for"; and that is why, lastly, the Word among us is only a promise and a vigilant prophecy of the invisible. From Seir, a voice calls to the prophet:[17] "Watchman, what of the night? Watchman, what of the night? The watchman said, The morning cometh, and also the night: if ye will enquire, enquire ye: return, come."

The form of the world is duration, and this is the form of sin, the refusal of the eternal moment—time, succession, and desire.[18] It is the postponement of the act and the retreat from God; it is the doubt which is interposed between knowing and doing; it is the cowardice of the man who rests upon his works and judges them, his covenant with the serpent. In what strange and secret ways time is linked to sin only the sinner knows, in the

[17] Isaiah, XXI, 11–12.

[18] When Schopenhauer writes: "Time has its origin not in things but in the conscious subject," we again find this definition of time as refusal of the moment and of the immediate submission to the word. But the resemblance is only a formal one. The time Kierkegaard suffers from is engendered by the sinner's anguish, while Schopenhauer's time is the "ideality" of the conscious subject, a spiritualist chimera, a nostalgia. That is why Kierkegaard's time can experience a redemption by the act, whereas Schopenhauer's fades into pure absence.

moment of faith, when by grace he can break this bond. "If ye will enquire, enquire ye." But the answer is: "Return. Come." (Convert, in the Douay Bible.) In the light that springs out of the act of faith, the mystery of time is unveiled; but a new time takes its course, and its measure is still more mysterious. Thus: the pardoned sinner lives in time as against the current of his duration, lives from act to act. And his time is no longer his sin but, we might say, his patience. For he stands where God has put him, and this is no longer a drifting with the current. He lives in the form of the world, but he is that which transforms it. Passion of the "Christian life," this matter of God in time, this matter of eternity!

"It requires a purely human courage to renounce time in order to gain eternity: for I gain it and can no longer renounce it for all eternity; and that is the paradox; but it requires a paradoxical and humble courage to embrace time by virtue of the absurd.[19] And this courage is the courage of faith. By faith, Abraham did not lose Isaac; it is by faith first of all that he received *him*."[20]

## v    The Time of the Act Is Rebirth, Initiation

Between birth and death all man's reality is in his act. Every act is transition and tension—transition from death to life, tension between what resists and what

---

[19] Kierkegaard means: by virtue of this inconceivable paradox, the historical Incarnation of God. There is no rational answer to Saint Anselm's *Cur Deus Homo?*
[20] *Fear and Trembling.*

creates, victory of the Word over the flesh, authority of
the person over the individual anarchy.

It is here that we approach the mystery, without which
all would be absurd: the act destroys time, since it is at
the same moment both life and death of the beings and
things it promotes to existence; but destroying time, it
recreates and redeems it, since it supplies a measure and
a rhythm by linking time to personal destiny. Thus the
absolute act would be absolute creation, but an act of
man is never anything but a redemption—a theologian's
distinction, intended to forestall pride. But the vision of
the man who acts is not a judgment of results, of
creatures, nor is it an estimation of causes. The act is
never a consequence; it is always an initiation. The vision
of the man who acts is entirely absorbed by the moment,
by the transition from what dies to what is born—by
reality.

"He who must act, if he seeks to judge himself according to the successes he achieves, will never undertake
anything. Even if his success delighted the whole world,
it would be of no use to the hero; for the hero has known
his success only when all was over; and it is not by success that he was a hero, but by his undertaking."[21]

The time of the act is recorded upon the features of
the heroic countenance. In this flesh that can grow old,
the tension of life and death has set victorious signs.
What is the person? The hero's vision and visage, his
vision *against* his visage, his vision that *creates* his visage.
The visage belongs to time, but the vision belongs to the

[21] *Works of Love.*

word from which it proceeds; and if a man's face is
beautiful, it is because it is an act and a destiny, a
signature of history, an effigy of the creative Word.

## VI   THE CONTRARY OF THE ACT IS DESPAIR

We know this as we know we must die: without
believing it. In truth, we have every reason to doubt it,
if it is true that doubt is revolt and that in order to admit
it to ourselves, we must have the joy which is born from
the act of faith. When Kierkegaard wrote his treatise on
*The Sickness unto Death,*[22] he had in fact just transcended this illusion of despair, which consists in imagining that the act is a human power—whence the impossi-
bility of risking it.

A man in the grip of faith realizes that the act is the
contrary of despair. But he *knows* it altogether differently than the despairing man *imagines* it. Because the
relation of despair to the act is not only a reversal but
an irreversible creation. And this results from the nature
of the act, better still, from its origin. This results from
the absolute of the person initiating the act.

The man in despair, the doubter, or simply the man
without faith, the weakened, vague, and feverish man
who peoples our cities, the faceless, neighborless—and
vocationless!—man imagines that the act will come as a
leap of joy, a revolt, a desperate affirmation of his pride,
as the proof, finally, of his self; yet he knows that he has

[22] "This sickness is not unto death, but for the glory of God. . . ."
John XI, 4.

no self, or that his self is despair; that is, that he does not believe in it and that he believes in no act. He lives in desire and in nostalgia, and his gaze is not a vision of reality, but a way of casting an eye upon the "others," upon the custom of the city.

How could this man perform an act? For the act is decision, rupture, isolation, when the very being of the man in despair consists of his bonds, his belief with the mass in the reality of the others in the totality. How could this man perform an act? For the act is immediate, creation and initiation, that is, pure sobriety; whereas the very being of the man in despair is a calculation ceaselessly distorted by the terror of losing what he does not even possess. Thus the absolute act, if he imagines it, would be his death, and that is why he does not believe in it. No one escapes the form of the world, but to endure it is indeed to despair. One must then— recreate it?

"Man can do only one thing in complete sobriety: the absolute."[23]

Between the man in despair and the absolute there is all the romanticism which desires the act to be power; there is that *self* of desire that seeks to seize the act: the moment! But the absolute which touches our lives moves us because it is an order, a Word received from elsewhere; a rupture of any human drama we could anticipate, desire, and describe; a rupture and a vision.

The presence of the absolute in the moment's perfect and insentient sobriety is the submission to the Word of

[23] *Richtet selbst.*

God, the prophecy in the immediate. What has happened? Now I am alone upon the way, but I see faces where before only a crowd stirred.

We see no face except in the act of loving.

## VII   EVERY VOCATION IS UNPRECEDENTED

For it is, in fact, prophecy—and it is from prophecy alone that reality and seriousness proceed, the risk and splendor of a man's life. Man distinguishes himself from the monkey in that he prophesies, solely and from the beginning. This is why man has a visage and a vision, which the animals do not have; and this is why man is heroic.

Here we must note a remarkable characteristic: Kierkegaard has spoken very little *of* vocation.[24] This is because he *speaks* his vocation, and never distinguishes himself *from* it. Yet there is no doubt that he was aware of this particular aspect of his destiny, which in fact qualifies the vocation: the *improbable*.

Are not his bitterest castigations of the "Christianity of Christendom," of this "inconceivable illusion of the senses" addressed precisely to the doctrinal "probability"

[24] Nonetheless, in the *Journal* for 1846–1848 we find some notations of this kind: "Great will be my responsibility if I reject a mission of this kind," that is, if he rejects his mission as a religious writer to become a country pastor, for example. This, he says, is because his orders are to "stand fast in suffering." The country presbytery would be an easy solution, particularly with regard to the sufferings he knows all too well his attacks against the "established church" will cause him.

of a religion brought within the reach of the "mass," whereas the true faith is that of the solitary whom nothing sustains except faith?

"He who does not renounce probability never enters into relation with God. Religious audacity, a fortiori Christian audacity, is beyond all probability, precisely where probability is renounced."[25] Because we must create our way, not follow it; because the act initiates; because man's dignity is to advance into the invisible and to prophesy "by virtue of the absurd."

Man can only be determined by his God or by the "world"; the choice must be made. One must be a Christian or a Philistine. The Philistine is the man without vocation. He does not believe in the act; and he dies by chance, without having encountered anyone, including himself.[26] He lives in the form of the world; and it is not that this form is particularly real for him, it is only the least improbable. But the Christian who advances into the new is aware only of what he transforms. His knowledge is act and prophetic vision. The measurement of the time of his life resides only in the vocation he incarnates. On the Way that begins at his feet, he never dies by accident or surprise, and not because he has known the day and the hour but because he knows the *moment*, if he lives

[25] *Richtet selbst.*

[26] What is particularly distressing about bourgeois existence is that it is entirely determined until death, but that death occurs as an absurdity, the first in its history, but decisive. To an inquiry "on the most important encounter of your life," M. Clément Vautel, spokesman for the bourgeois, replied: "I have never met anyone. [*Je n'ai jamais rencontré personne.*]"

by the Word. On account of the eternal moment, *the hero always dies before he dies.*[27] This is the last secret of the act, and the seal of Christian love.


## 3   *Necessity of the Solitary*

### I   WE CALL SPIRIT . . .

What is the complaint of Intelligence? According to the writings most worthy of formulating its opinion, and which are full of bitter protests against mass rule and the various outrages incurred by the individual, the anonymous Powers and the Standard are enthroned, and this at the expense of the human. In the midst of this crisis, considered as unprecedented, what is the individual doing to protect himself? And what claims does he make upon existence? For it is excellent to defend one's self, especially when it possesses more reality than anonymity. But again, this self must have some basis. This is not self-evident, so to speak; Marxists and Fascists deny it more passionately than the bourgeois affirm it. On the one hand we see a faith, on the other a bad humor—and some think, a bad conscience.

What do the collectivists say? that the great number is more precious than the small; that the life of the spirit is possible only if we have first assured the other life, the physical conditions of existence; that justice lies in the equality of all, and virtue in public opinion; that history "evolves" according to inevitable laws, and that the desire

[27] *Fear and Trembling.*

of individuals will change nothing; that a revolt, finally, of one against the many would be the sign of a dreadful pride if, first of all, it did not evidence a ridiculous lack of practicality.

And what do our authors say since the nineteenth century? The same phrases, almost, *but with reservations,* that is, without seriously believing in them, or at least without proving by the fact that they believe in them. It would then be a matter of believing in something which legitimates this skepticism or this "measure . . ." Otherwise the faith of some will inevitably triumph over the defensive bad humor of others. Of course, this has been thought of. The boldest speak of restoring "spirit" its place . . . But *what* spirit? And who let it be lost? And what is to be sacrificed to it?

Suppose that a man appears and that he accepts the collectivist challenge. He maintains that the solitary is greater than the anonymous crowd; that the life of the spirit is possible only if one has first renounced the other life; that the laws of history are nothing if the act of man contradicts them; that the faith of one man is stronger, in his humility and before God—for it is *faith*—than the realist's speeches and popular enthusiasm; that justice, finally, and virtue have no reality if each is not in its place, where the vocation of God has put it.

Let us suppose such a man exists. What will we do with him, with this hero—is he not?—of the spiritual values which in fact we profess to defend? Kierkegaard's biography will give us the answer. We shall begin by calling his seriousness into doubt. "Who is Doctor Søren Kierkegaard? A man totally lacking in seriousness," we read in a newspaper of the period. We shall make fun of his physical appearance—his trousers are too long. We shall show without too much difficulty that his ideas are designed to make life impossible, since they imply the martyrdom of the good Christians, as if religion, for all eternity, were not on the contrary the wisest way of enduring the evils of this world! The Church, by the voice of its bishops, will try to prove that Kierkegaard is talking nonsense; some will suggest that he be forbidden access to the church; public opinion will unanimously condemn his mad pride; has he not written that the press is in our time the decisive obstacle to the preaching of true Christianity? Exhausted by this long, disproportionate effort against his time, overwhelmed by general reprobation, he will die in the hospital, saying to his only friend: "Greet all mankind! I loved them greatly . . ."

This happened in Copenhagen in 1855. Since then, it is true, things have changed. One might even say that they have grown worse, but we must avoid suggesting to our contemporaries that this worse cannot be aggravated, however little they surrender to it.

## II  WHAT IS SPIRIT?

Thus, we hear talk of rescuing the spirit. What is spirit? "Spirit is the power a man's knowledge exerts upon his life."[28] It is not knowledge, it is not power, but the power of knowledge in practice. Let us not suppose this is casuistry; autonomous knowledge, or power, wins decora-

[28] *Journal*, vol. X.

tions for its possessor, but the effective practice of knowledge can lead to ruin or even, perhaps, to martyrdom. So let us not be hasty to defend the "rights" of spirit; it is not a distinction. And who among us can say that he has calculated the expense?

We must know of what we speak, and this may not be possible unless we know where we are going. Where does Kierkegaard's thought lead? Against the press and public opinion, he protests in favor of what is "original"; against the passion of multitudes, he champions the mysterious charity of irony; against History, he posits the act of the man responsible for his fate. But doesn't all this lead to martyrdom in the world being prepared for us? It may, if God wills it. Kierkegaard's demand is limited to the moment of choice, when man sets out, "by virtue of the absurd," on the way God shows him—alone.

This priority of faith over the truths favoring life, this primary solitude before God—is this what the defenders of spiritual priority advocate? Spirit is drama, attack; and risk. And we may doubt whether those who castigate materialism in the name of the values they have been unable to protect or to sacrifice further really believe in spirit. They declare too belatedly that "money doesn't make happiness," and that there exist other possessions no violence can affect, but this is a pathetic answer to the revolt of the poor whom they fear more than they love. . . .

If we truly desired a champion of the spirit, we should do well to find him among those for whom spirit needs no defense, among those who merely bear witness to its incarnation; we should do well to apply to those for whom spirit is not a kind of comfort but an absolute adventure, a judgment of man: thus Pascal, Nietzsche, Dostoevski. We might mention several others. What have they in common then, aside from genius? Perhaps only their suffering. But if there is no hierarchy possible in these matters, sacrifice here takes the place of measurement, since it is an incontestable act. Such is the new greatness, the new measurement of spirit. Thus we shall choose this great solitary, this extreme and decisive witness, whose death, like a seal of eternity, attested in its plenitude to the primacy of the spiritual act: Kierkegaard.

The great disease of the age, and the terror our false gods are beginning to sow within it, have weakened some minds, as is evidenced by the renaissance, or better the discovery, among us of this pitiless thought.

A harsh remedy? We had to feel sick indeed to call upon the severe physician which the less-depressed health of another century had killed. Further, it has become possible to grasp, in the development of the most significant features of our period, the truth of the anathema with which Kierkegaard greeted their birth. We turn toward this prophet of our miseries; we return to the point of origin where he stands; we place in him our hope of finding another way, a path which leads neither to Rome nor Berlin, to Geneva nor Moscow, but to ourselves before God.

Søren Kierkegaard is doubtless the capital thinker of our period; I mean, the most absolute, the most fundamental objection raised against it, a literally embarrassing figure, an almost unendurable reminder of the presence *in these times* of the eternal. For it is not enough to applaud his theses to appease that piercing gaze; and if we are deaf to his voice, how hush up the scandal of his death, which defines the fate of spirit among us? If public opinion killed Kierkegaard, it has had no hold on the sarcasms with which he stigmatized it, though they are more charitable than the discourses in honor of progress; for the sole honor of our age will be, perhaps, by a mysterious compensation, to have understood better than any other the message of the "solitary before God."

III  IRONY

When I see the ironic features of Kierkegaard's great countenance reappearing through the confusion of doctrines all over Europe, an image occurs to me whose absurdity would not have displeased the Danish philosopher's Shakespearean humor. It is the image of the Chesire Cat in *Alice in Wonderland*. Recall that enormous and subversive creature, whose laughter has the gift of exasperating the Queen. She storms and shrieks her favorite imprecation: "Off with his head!" Then the Cat rises into the air and gradually makes its body invisible; only its grinning face remains above the outraged executioners, who refuse to cut off such a head. Finally the Cat vanishes completely. But at certain moments, it chooses to reappear. *Its grin shows first of all,* nothing but its immaterial grin floating on high. Then, just the head recomposes around this disturbing apparition. The laughter of Kierkegaard floating over our age!

In a world of mass rule the heaviest kind of seriousness also prevails. We do not laugh in the dictator's presence, nor in the ranks of the assault troops. If laughter is the characteristic of man, we have become inhuman indeed. It seems that each of us bears the weight of the world and the century's dark future. The modern clerk has been described as overwhelmed by all the miseries of the age, of which he feigns to believe himself either the victim or the cause.[29] This man whom history terrorizes, who takes refuge in public concerns, as we might see a film to forget our troubles in a fictional drama, this man whose morning newspaper alarms him more than the abyss of his own soul, Kierkegaard describes as "infinitely comical." We must risk this expression: the laughter of charity. "Christianity has discovered a misery whose existence man ignores, as man; and it is the sickness unto death (sin).[30] Let the natural man draw up an exhaustive list of the horrible, the Christian laughs at the total!" Why this scandalous laughter? Because "the infinite fear of a single danger would make all other dangers nonexistent for us."

But can this fear of a single danger still seriously characterize the average Christian of our times? It is here that Kierkegaard's irony turns its edge against the Chris-

---

[29] "Here, again, the modern clerk is a Protestant," adds M. Benda, who, as regards Protestants, knows only Renouvier.
[30] John, XI, 4, Jesus knows that Lazarus will die. What he wants the others to know is that the only sickness to be feared is sin.

tian world, against the world that allies itself with spirit
or which makes a profession of appealing to it. "The New
Testament resembles a satire on man. It contains consolations and more consolations for those who suffer on
account of Christ. It supposes, quite naïvely, that the
Christian suffers for his doctrine . . ." And that is the
tragi-comedy of the Christianity of Christendom. Poor
average Christian, what have you suffered for your
doctrine? You suffer, it is true, but is it not precisely for
those things that your doctrine shows you are vain? Yet
you must choose. *Either* you believe in the unique grace
of God, in the infinite abyss where you find yourself, *or*
you also believe in the seriousness of the existence symbolized by the quotations of the Bourse. *Either* you stake
your whole life on forgiveness, *or* you rest on your virtue
as well. *Either* you see that the burning question is to
know whether you yourself are a Christian, *or* you
vituperate the Godless Russians. But do you know what
you are suffering from? From your sin, or from that of
others? Ah, the bitter and infinite comicality of this
"believer," who trembles for the fate of spirit in the world,
and for his fate in the world without spirit, exactly as if
spirit did not exist! Shall we be witnesses or apprehensive
spies? Shall we forever wait for the "wakening of the
mass" to affirm that all its gods are false gods? But are
they false gods for us? Are we really appealing to spirit?
No, we are appealing to the "spiritual realm," which is
much less dangerous; everybody will belong to it.

"Two questions," Kierkegaard says, "bear witness to
spirit: 1) Is what is preached to us possible? 2) Can I

do it? Two questions bear witness to the absence of spirit: 1) Is it real? 2) Has my neighbor Christofersen done it? Has he really done it?"[31]

We still ask the last question. We do not believe in spirit; we prefer not to make a scandal; we really believe in public opinion. We read the newspapers, that is our reality. On Sunday we sometimes go to church to deplore the world's atheism. "The New Testament supposes, quite naïvely, that the Christian suffers for his doctrine . . . (No, he merely suffers because not everyone has accepted it) . . . and offers its consolation; and on this text sermons are preached to us, who have not wanted to suffer."

"In the sumptuous church appears the venerable and noble Court Chaplain, the Society favorite; he appears before an assembly of the elite, and preaches with emotion on this text which he has chosen himself: God has elected the meek and the despised in the world—and no one laughs."[32]

Then Kierkegaard's laughter rings out. It is not the laughter of a Molière; Molière makes the crowd laugh at the expense of the extravagant character. But Kierkegaard laughs at the crowd, at its theatrical and fervent seriousness, and at its fear of all extravagance. "You may make them do whatever you desire, good or evil, and only one condition matters to them: that they be always like the others, that they imitate—and never act alone." But what God demands is precisely the opposite: He

[31] *Stages on Life's Way.*
[32] *The Present Moment.*

wants originality. "That is why the Word of God is such that we are always being shown some passage that contradicts another." For the appearance of contradiction obliges us to choose, gives faith its place, and constrains us to originality. "After all, professors and disciples are comfortable only in imitation; that is why they have united within it so touchingly, and that is what they call love."[33]

The solitary's laughter, which perhaps resembles the enigmatic pity of a Dostoevski—here Kierkegaard's countenance is recomposed entire. And we see that his laughter is nothing but the sorrow of the witness to the Spirit, amid the crowd.

IV   ORIGINALITY

What does he mean by this word originality? We must locate its meaning at the very center of his thought, or better of his action. This center is "the category of the solitary." Many misinterpretations are possible here; let us avoid, from the start, three words which distort everything: anarchy, romanticism, individual. We need merely confront them with the Christian reality of man. The solitary to whom Kierkegaard appeals is man isolated before his God. But how could this be, except by the effect of faith? God must summon him, name him, and thereby separate him; otherwise man is nothing but an instance of the herd. The solitary before God is the man who answers to the summons of faith. When we speak of romanticism,

[33] *Journal.*

of anarchy, of individualism, we refer in every case to revolt, but to a revolt that is ultimately imaginary. For the order of this world is itself in revolt against the received order of God, which will be the Order of the Kingdom. And to negate a negation is to be swallowed up in the abyss of nothingness. Only the Christian's revolt is a position: obedience. And if God's summons isolates a man from the world, it is because the world, in its fallen form, is opposed to the world as God created it, is opposed to the transformation Spirit seeks, is opposed to Order. "And be not conformed to this world: but be ye transformed," says Saint Paul.

The solitary before God is the man who takes a position *at the origin* of his reality. Such a man can judge this world, and determine himself in it as not being determined. There is no other "reaction" against the age, no other creative revolution. And all our appeals to spirit, if they are not this return to the Real, are merely pursuit of the wind, defection, or fantastic pride.

v  THE SOLITARY AND THE FALSE GODS

We believe in the mob, in race, in history (or rather in the evolution of societies), in revolution, in capital, in the judgment of public opinion; we believe in the past, in the collective, in the future; and all this is nothing but evasion of our eternal present, all this is only mythology. The gods of the age have the existence we attribute to them; alas, it would be false to say that they have none.

But once again, we do not escape the public chimeras by

eloquently denouncing them by virtue of an idea of man which pagan reason readily admits: aggressive Nietzscheanism or demoniac despair seeking identity "out of hatred for existence and according to its misery." This revolt is not based on the effective transformation of the world. It still participates in degradation. "A truly wicked objection always turns against what has raised it."[34] And he who resorts to his rebellious self against the forces of annihilation establishes himself upon nothingness and precipitates his own ruin.

The solitary who condemns the mass can establish himself only upon his vocation; and he can find identity only by the divine right of the Word that distinguishes him. Supreme humility of the solitary! *He can compare himself only to the vocation he receives.* Where would pride find a purchase in a being so simplified that he is nothing more than obedience—insofar as he acts—and penitence—insofar as his vocation transcends him?

If Kierkegaard condemns the crowd, it is not that he fears it, or fears losing in it the wretched ego of the psychologists. His reproach of the crowd is that it demands nothing from him. The crowd wants us all to be simply irresponsible; thereby we flatter it, and it recognizes us as its own. The crowd is the meeting place of men evading themselves and their vocation. It belongs to none, and thereby draws its assurance in crime.

"There was not found a single soldier who dared lay hands on Caius Marius, such is the truth. But three or

[34] *The Sickness unto Death.*

four women, in the illusion of being a crowd and thinking that no one could say which of them had done the
thing or had begun it, these women would have had such
courage! O falsehood!" The mob is nothing but *each
man's* evasion of responsibility for his act. "For a crowd
is an abstraction, which has no hands, but each isolated
man has, in the nature of things, two hands, and when
he lays these two hands on Marius, they are his hands
and not those of his neighbor and not those of the crowd,
which has no hands." Alone before Christ, would a man
dare advance and spit in the face of the Son of God? But
if he is of a crowd, he will have this "courage"; he has
had it.

We must go further. The crowd is not only in the
street. It is in the thoughts of the men of this age. Kierkegaard's realistic genius was able to expose it in the
deepest intimacy of the individual existence.

Each time we say of one of our gods that he is powerful, we testify to our resignation. The crowd has no other
existence and no other power than *my* refusal to exist
before God and to wield the power that I am. The crowd
is merely *my* degradation. And all the sciences that study
historical or sociological laws are as an inversion of
theology, a theology of degradation.

Kierkegaard's opposition to Hegel here assumes its
profoundest and most immediate significance. Hegel
objectivized everything: Spirit, history, dialectics, finally
man himself in the eyes of man. He sought to eliminate
from the world the ultimate paradox and scandal of the
solitary. He wanted everything to be explained, to follow,

in order that the scandalous possibility of the free acts of
providence be banished forever. The undertaking might
be regarded as magnificent if mass man did not today
seek to manipulate it for a blood cult to his false gods.

Mass man has not read Hegel, of course, but Hegel
is in all our newspapers; Hegel dominates Marxism and
fascism; he dominates the atheology of the sociologists,
of the historians, of the bourgeois clerks. How escape
him? Who has really tried, save Kierkegaard, alone of
his stature? Some flee into the future, others into the past;
but who would stand in the moment, "in the sight of the
Lord," as the Christians say? (Is this easy? Or even
possible? Is it an effect of our choice or a moment of our
life? They speak of it easily enough, the Christians.)

A few atheists have seen the danger here, but without
seeing man in the present order of his sin, nor in the
coming order of grace. Thus Maurras, when he de-
nounces the myths of social Hegelianism: "The best
means of being free of them will be to reconsider their
origin. *To conceal the certain present, they mortgage the
future,* but to win this last security, the habits of the religious spirit make them conceive a World Soul which
they imagine (though with neither frankness nor exactitude) as a kind of invisible and monster vertebrate,
mysteriously distributed and vaporized in things in order
to answer (how and why?) our desires. This kind of crude,
completely unintelligible providence is the simple suc-
cedaneum of intelligible supernatural providence."[35] But

---

[35] *Le Chemin du Paradis* (translator's italics).

who could fail to see that this World Soul also conditions our critic, and even in his skepticism, when he proclaims after Auguste Comte: "The dead govern the living." Talk about a mortgage on the future! For if the dead govern the living, it is because none of the living dares live. And how live, if not by the summons of providence? And how obey that summons if we pose conditions: "intelligible supernatural providence!"

Omnipotence of the rationalist pretensions! "The best way of freeing oneself from them will be to reconsider their origin." Only Kierkegaard can designate it for us; it is in the modern rejection of "category of the solitary," of the man who lives on the Word alone, between tenses, in the eternal moment.

VI  CAN THE SOLITARY ACT?

The Hegelian witchcraft is objectivity: that attitude of the man who no longer seeks to be the *subject* of his action, who abandons it to the laws of Evolution. Kierkegaard, on the contrary, repeats: *Subjectivity is truth.* Man's freedom and dignity are the consequences of the fact that he is the only subject of his life. But he must be careful not to understand the expression in the romantic sense. *I* am the *subject,* but it remains to be discovered where this *I* comes from, how it *can* act. Must it be an imperialism of the pure ego, as Fichte so madly dreamed? If this is the case, I have no problem. This "pure ego" does not involve my despair. Of course, I can dream my ideal perfection; I can dream my vocation and its dan-

gers. . . . Kierkegaard waits for us upon our awakening.
He seizes us precisely when all the systems collapse before the terror of the concrete choice. Now, you shall
witness to the power which your knowledge exerts over
your life. You thought you were a *self;* witness to the fact
that you are not a crowd, imitation and mere object of the
world's laws. The crowd waits; if you follow it, it will
scorn you, no doubt, but that is the common fate; you do
not run much of a risk. If you say no, if you act, it may
kill you; even if it decorates your "hero's" grave, the
final insult.[36] It is a question of knowing now in whose
name you will act, if you act. The first duty of a "pure
self" is to persevere in its active being; in this extremity,
compromise is justified. But if your self is not yours, if it
is a vocation received from *elsewhere,* and if you have
truly received it, you need no longer choose; your death
is behind you, it is no longer your concern, no longer your
anxiety. And above all, it is no longer that revolting
absurdity which nothing in the world could make acceptable, while the martyr receives his death with a kind
of sobriety.

Only the believer acts and only he *can* be the subject

[36] Why raise the question apropos of a case as exceptional as
martyrdom? For the purity of the vision. The inevitable reminder of the daily necessities is only a pretext of dread. If
daily life is so undramatic, this does not signify that the ultimate
questions never are raised in it, but simply that they are drowned
in it. Men prefer to "die imperceptibly," as Nietzsche said, and
this is what they call their "everyday life." This is perhaps nothing
more than a final crime of the "crowd" in our moral existence, a
question incorrectly put, *a blurred vision.*

of his action; but that is because he is, in the other sense of the term, subject to the Word living within him. It is in this sense that Kierkegaard's formula is pure; only this total *subjection* is active.

It is also being-in-the-world, presence. In our mass age, the "solitary before God" is also the man who is most real, most present. Because he knows that there exists an "elsewhere," and that the eternal comes into contact with him, he can agree to live *hic et nunc* to the end, while the crowd is ubiquity and endless evasion into the past or the future.

VII   ONE ALONE USEFUL TO ALL

Carlyle has a famous phrase summarizing Bentham's utilitarianism: "Given a world of fools, to prove that virtue is the result of their collective aspirations." Reversing this relation, it would remain for me to prove concerning Kierkegaard that his "category of the solitary" is the only practical basis of a truly vital collectivity. Yet it is wiser to refrain from insisting on such a reinstatement. For two reasons, I believe. Who, first of all among us, would dare assert that this category is so familiar to him that he can consider it as given? There is a strong temptation to shift from a criticism of illusory collectivities to the utopia of a Christian community, by the indispensable but perhaps also quite formal artifice of isolation before God. On the other hand, the act of "the solitary" is not an act whose consequences we need develop. Either *it is,* and it is the act of God, or else I imagine it, and my discourse is vain.

For the man who anticipates in its brutal reality, in its ultimate seriousness and its absolute risk, the nature of the solitude to which Kierkegaard has testified, it no longer appears necessary to refute the objections of the "social sense." Several of Kierkegaard's works bear this famous dedication: "To the solitary, whom I call with joy and gratitude: my reader." Kierkegaard knew that when one speaks to all or against all, each man believes that the others are meant, and no one considers himself addressed; but if one speaks to the solitary of his dread, it is of mine.

Kierkegaard addresses the Christian as the only responsible man among us. He knows that in all ages, the misery of the times does not result from the fact that it is "without God," but from the fact that it is without masters, that is, without martyrs to instruct it. It is to the salt that we must restore the savor; it is the salt alone that we may reproach for being insipid. Nothing will ever be real for all, if it is not first real for one alone.

Now, we must be the impossible: We must be the solitary. Can Kierkegaard help us? Or has he only delivered us from our last excuses, from our last uncertainties as to Spirit's nature and concrete demands? Yet must he not have known great succors in order to dare show us the vanity of *all* ours? *Somnium narrare vigilantis est,* Seneca says. The total admission of our despair alone bears witness to consolation.

*—1934*

# Franz Kafka, or the Acknowledgment of Reality

Franz Kafka was born in Prague in 1883 and spent most of his life in that city. After taking his doctorate in law, he worked first for a general insurance firm, then for one specializing in workers' insurance. He also tried his hand in a carpentry shop, and for some time apprenticed himself to a truck-gardening venture. When he decided to emigrate to Berlin in order to devote himself at last to his writing, he was already doomed by tuberculosis of the larynx, of which he died in Vienna in 1924.

Kafka published only a small number of stories during his lifetime. But among his papers were found the almost complete manuscripts of three novels: *The Trial, The Castle,* and *Amerika.* The vision of the world they afford has an agonizing exactitude. He considers our everyday life with a minuteness it can scarcely endure. The state of extreme lucidity which this vision provokes in us resembles a nightmare down to the last detail. But whereas so many poets at the same period were trying to rave methodically, Kafka continually brings us back, with a kind of inflexible humor, to the *soberest* awareness of our human condition. It is as if he incited his heroes to a kind of sabotage of bourgeois existence: by dint of conscientiousness, character, and exactitude in the exercise of life's ordinary functions and social relations they discover its fundamental incoherence. But then, everything becomes strangely significant. The merest event gradually swells to the proportions of a parable of existence. Or, conversely, starting from an inexplicable and monstrous[1] event occurring in the life of his hero, Kafka convinces us that the details of everyday existence, and the feeling of strangeness that at times accompanies it under the surface, are to be explained in the most "logical" manner, once we refer them to this mysterious initial fact of extravagant aspect. Behind this psychology of everyday anguish, we sense in Kafka certain religious intentions and the *quest*, at least, for a theology. All of this, not expressed but veiled and betrayed only by certain pecularities of the narrative. . . .

Kafka's favorite reading and his social preoccupations, as his biographer Max Brod describes them, may help us to divine the nature of his enigmatic intent. His passion for moral absolutes is typically Jewish, but his psychology of anguish is evidently inspired by Kierkegaard, whom he was one of the first to discover in the twentieth century. Further, his impulse to sobriety, to the education of spiritual forces by practical and social activity is no less certainly related to his admiration for Goethe. Nothing is more suggestive than this meeting in one man of two such contradictory and, in so many respects, exclusive influences. I take it as a special opportunity to confront, in the quick of an existence, the spiritual adventures described in the preceding pages.

[1] For example, Gregor Samsa's sudden transformation into an unspecified creature, probably a gigantic bedbug, in *Metamorphosis,* or the obscure charge that weighs on the hero of *The Trial.*

*1*   The Trial, *or the law that leads to death*

I am not sure if *The Trial* is Kafka's masterpiece, but it is difficult to imagine a book more profound. One even has the sense, reading it, of reading for the first time an absolutely profound book. Not that it claims to pass beyond the appearances of this world into esotericism; on the contrary, it confines itself to describing these appearances with a realism adequate to lay bare their objective incoherence, at the same time that it refuses any reassuring interpretation, that is, all the conventions auspiciously introduced by men in order to "act as if" their lives were justified in themselves.

Joseph K., a bank clerk, is arrested one morning by two detectives, who inform him that he is indicted; but they do not know for what and are not authorized to know. Then he is released. The entire story concerns not the trial, which never takes place, but the trial's preliminaries, the attempts of the accused to clarify his situation in the eyes of an unreachable, infinitely pedantic juridical machinery whose offices are located in wretched districts of the city or in attics. Joseph K. never manages to reach the highest authorities; moreover, no one has been able to do so. On the last page, he is killed, but in conditions too depressing for him even to dream of resisting.

The story takes place in the pallid reality of a modern city, perhaps lightly distorted, here and there, by swift expressionist touches. We must be careful not to assume that the author has indulged himself in a mystery whose key he has resolved to keep from us. *The Trial* is not an allegory. Joseph K. asks all the questions the rational reader will ask. Sometimes he protests—cautiously. But the justice that pursues him is not the kind from which one extricates oneself by accepting or even by rejecting its demands. *The Trial* would be a revolting book if it were not first of all overwhelming. It is quite a lot like life.

Kafka's realism has nothing in common with what textbooks or newspapers call realism. There is no question of showing, for instance, that scurrilousness is the best way to succeed, nor of suggesting that a laborer's ideas have more reality than the vapors of a heroine in a bourgeois novel. Kafka's realism resides in the sobriety of his vision; and it is ultimately his vision itself which is the book's true subject. The almost unendurable precision with which he reports certain banal conversations could only have been achieved by means of a *suspension of judgment*, which is in itself the whole drama of *The Trial*: an assertion of reality and at the same time, whenever a rebellious impulse appears, an assertion of the absolute vanity of any judgment, of any taking sides, of any act.

All of men's efforts—including those of the philosophers—are perhaps only attempts to escape this vision, which is anguish itself. Means sometimes childish, sometimes subtle to elude the *mad* seriousness of real life, to liken it to a game from which it would be possible to break free, insofar as one might know its rules. Thus, one is tempted to relate Kafka's vision to that of the dream. And it is true that the complicity which, in *The*

*Trial,* links judges, lawyers, and accused is a characteristic feature of the anxiety dream. But if Kafka or his hero were only dreamers, there would then remain one escape: to wake up. And the *final* seriousness of the situation would disappear. I do not believe that Kafka lived in another world than our own. At most, in another vision, that of man "arrested," precisely, that of the man who thinks and lives in the suspension of judgment. Joseph K. has seen the world before acting, and remains a prisoner of this vision, which will henceforth permit him only a temporary freedom. We are all arrested; it would be better to know as much; for we could then know that there is really no way to save ourselves. (Unless a hand is extended to us from elsewhere, unless someone loves and "calls" us, addresses a vocation to us . . .)

Now, to acknowledge the ultimate seriousness, the absolute tragic nature of our condition, to acknowledge that *we cannot wake up* from this universal nightmare, we must have transcended the level of this life, if only once, in the lightning flash of a presentiment. Just as the whole extent of the ravages of capitalism cannot be judged except from a revolutionary point of view, so the scandal of life cannot be seriously judged except from a somehow anti-vital viewpoint, or a transcendent one. There are no acknowledgments except of the past, in other words: of the by-passed. This is why Kafka's novel supposes, by the mere fact that it exists, a kind of revelation, an "elsewhere" at least suggested, which we would have to rediscover beyond the lacunae of reality.

Of what nature was the transcendence which conditioned Kafka's vision.

In an appendix to *The Trial,* Max Brod tells us how he was obliged to wrest from Kafka the writings which his friend refused to publish, including this novel. What were Kafka's scruples? "He wanted his work to be on a scale with his religious preoccupations," we are told. And criticism, embarrassed, overlooks this or turns to psychologizing. But to pass this over in silence is here equivalent to a complicity with the unqualified lawyers and negligent judges of *The Trial,* with all those who refuse to ask the ultimate questions, to demand that the last word be spoken.

Knowing almost nothing about Kafka, after a first reading of *The Trial* I had asked myself this question: Is it pure chance if Christian theology accounts for almost all the situations of this book? Is it pure chance if it offers us the formulas that seem most capable of summarizing the principal peripities of this enormous judiciary action? I say, summarize, for a thousand concrete details escape this interpretation. But if we retain only a general sense, the unforgettable atmosphere of a nightmare recollected the day after, then a kind of dogmatic schema appears.

Every man who has known the existence of the law knows himself condemnable, whatever he may do: "There is none righteous, no, not one," says Scripture. Whether we know it or not, we have all erred; and we are all, potentially, accused; this point of departure of *The*

*Trial* is found in the epistles of Saint Paul.[2] Who then is
the pitiless Judge? He is the God who gave the law, the
God of the Jews in whose "sight shall no man living be
justified." Why does He remain inaccessible? Because He
abides in heaven, and we are on earth; the supreme
authority exists and deliberates beyond all our imagining.
How could we speak to Him, and what would it avail
us to justify ourselves? In this state of tragic impotence
we are ready to grasp the smallest hint as to the nature
of the mystery. Here are the shyster lawyers who say they
know the secrets of justice. They do not precisely inspire
confidence, but who knows? We have no right to neglect
this slight and humiliating opportunity. And gradually we
come to suspect that they are in league with the Judge!
At least, they let us suspect as much. This is perhaps
another imposture. But from it they derive a kind of
prestige, and even one that is all the more magical, since
we have no means of verifying its basis in fact. Priests
and mages, last supports of man against God! In truth,
they are impotent, accused themselves, and ill-informed.

Need we carry the analogy further? This state of the
accused at liberty in universal complicity reminds me of
the "misery of man," not "without God" but delivered
to a God of Whom he can know only the wrath, and not
the mercy. It is the state of a man who knows that God
exists, but who can no longer obey Him, and who does
not know how to reach him, since he does not know the
"way" that links heaven and earth, since he does not
know Him who said: "*I am the way*."

[2] See Romans III, 10–20 and also Galatians.

Let us suppose, as a kind of counter-check, that Joseph K. believed in the Christ of the Gospels. The entire problematics of *The Trial* would then be set in motion again—and starting from the very point where Kafka's vision "arrested" it.

"No man cometh unto the Father, but by me." It is by the Son that God becomes for us the Father and ceases to be the remote Judge. But then acquittal is possible and grace may be granted! "I am the way," the Mediator has said. But then the act too is possible, and obedience practicable! Thus, faith in Christ is the way out, the possibility given man to walk, to escape "arrest." But it is also a result of this faith that we know our state—because it permits us to emerge from it—that we measure reality, and that we can acknowledge it.

Now here is the difficulty: I see in *The Trial* the veiled acknowledgment of our state; I see that this acknowledgment supposes at least the glimpse of a faith—and yet the novel ends by the hideous triumph of the law, that is, in the despair which is the recognized absence of faith. All that precedes can be taken as an illustration of the state of sin revealed by the moment of conversion. This vision of *man arrested* may be a background glance at humanity in revolt, which has lost the way; something analogous to the negative moment of an impulse—of a leap into the life of faith—the moment when the body gathers itself together and seems to refuse to leap in order to leap all the farther the moment after. But no, Kafka suspends the impulse. He knows he must leap, but at the last moment, he no longer *believes* that on the other side

he will land on solid ground. Thus he remains in an oppression of the spirit, an exhaustion of effort which no
act comes to fulfill.[3]

Here then is my hypothesis: Kafka's vision expresses
the situation of the man who is no longer sustained but
on the contrary obscurely *troubled* by a certain Christian
ambiance; to be exact: a Judeo-Christian ambiance. He
knows that God and His Justice exist; but he knows this
in a negative way, or, rather, he has a presentiment that
he has known it, and this suffices to waken an obscure
sense of guilt; but he has lost the confidence which
naïve periods of history (or of his own individual history) put in Revelation. Incapable of believing in it, he
represses it. And, henceforth, Revelation is no longer
what illuminates and reassures him, but what secretly dis-
quiets the reason and aggravates the awareness of anguish, that void in which man remains and cannot remain.
If faith were to supervene in his life, it would give him
the assurance of pardon. Then this obscure sense of guilt
could become distinct *consciousness of sin*, of the real
sin, which is much less a moral fault than the refusal to
love God in Christ. If faith supervened, Joseph K. would
abandon the vain efforts of a justification by his own

[3] Perhaps this image will suggest the spiritual cause of the state of
lassitude and frustration in which the heroes of *The Trial* are
kept. It is possible that the tuberculosis of which Kafka was to
die also played a certain part. Yet even supposing we were to
find in the works of authors suffering from this disease the same
atmosphere of oppression as in *The Trial*, we should still have
to explain why Kafka alone has been able to set in operation, in
such a significant way, this physiological predisposition.

moral means; he would know that acquittal is deserved only by the very man who renounces deserving it. The clear consciousness of sin is, in concrete terms, repentance can be provoked only by the certainty of forgiveness.

But, precisely, faith does not supervene. The obscure sense of guilt, which unceasingly persecutes the accused, does not lead to that clear consciousness of sin which only forgiveness can give us, nor to that certainty of forgiveness which only faith can give us. Joseph K. thus remains imprisoned in the mortal circle of the law. He recognizes, in all honesty, that man cannot emerge from the circle by himself.

There is, Kierkegaard said, "an infinite qualitative difference between God and man," so that no communication can be established from man to God, if one does not believe that it has been established, in the converse direction, from God to man, by the coming of Christ in history. Kafka *knew* that there must have been a way, and this was enough to make him cruelly conscious of the "arrest"; but he could not *believe* in the reality of this way, and that is why he refused to set out upon it. He demanded a previous certitude, which his strangely exact regard found nowhere in everyday life. For the way exists, as a truth of life, only for him who dares take a step upon it without seeing. But it eludes the eyes which seek to verify it in advance. This consciousness at the heart of anguish is a spiritual moment which we discover in every conversion. Kierkegaard has described it dialectically, from the point of view of a believer-in-spite-of-everything. Kafka isolates it and stops there (*arrested*) with a kind of meticulous, ironic, and despairing honesty.


## II   The Castle, *or enigmatic grace*

*The Castle* corresponds to *The Trial* as grace corresponds to justice. But justice was inexorable, grace thus remains uncertain. It is the conclusion of *The Trial* which determines the *données* of *The Castle* and which prevents its action from achieving any result.

"K.," this time, is a surveyor. He has been summoned to the Castle, which dominates a mountain village, probably to do some work relating to his trade. But he will never manage to meet the Count. The entire novel takes place in the village, and is confined to the scrupulous description of K.'s vain attempts to reach the Castle; then to obtain, at least, some communication with the Count; lacking this, with the stewards; and since this too appears to be virtually impossible, to acquire certain complicities among those whom he believes to be in relation with the offices of the Castle. Sometimes he receives a message emanating from one of these offices. He is congratulated on his work when he is desperate over his idleness; or else he is given hope, in vague terms, of a remote solution. Everything occurs in an atmosphere of meddlesome and peasant-like suspicion. And the soft snow that covers the landscape makes the slightest effort exhausting.

Here the symbolism is perhaps clearer and more precisely determinant than it was in *The Trial*. Not that each incident can be interpreted—many probably having no other purpose than to create an atmosphere both realistic and bewildering. But from this atmosphere, and from the general development of the narrative, a parable takes form. Further, Brod's commentary, published as a post-face to *The Castle*, brings my theological hypotheses close to certainty: "What is the meaning of this Castle with its strange documents, its impenetrable hierarchy of officials, its moods and trickeries, its demand for unconditional respect, unconditional obedience? Without excluding more specific interpretations, which may be completely valid but which are subsumed within this one, as the inner compartments of a Chinese puzzle are enclosed within the outer, this "Castle," to which K. never gains admission, to which he can never even get near, is much the same thing as what the theologians call "grace," the divine guidance of human destiny (the village); the effectual cause of all chances, mysterious dispensations, favors, and punishments; the unmerited and the unattainable; the "non liquet" written over the life of everybody. In *The Trial* and *The Castle*, then, are represented the two manifested forms of the Godhead (in the sense of the *Cabbala*): justice and grace.

Doubtless one might further clarify certain elements of the allegory; I see its key in Kierkegaard's work. The messages received from the Castle all have the characteristics of that other message, which is the Bible, according to Kierkegaard: It will always be permissible to doubt their authenticity; we do not even know their exact date; and yet it happens that each man may read them as if he were dealing with letters written precisely to him, though their contents remain quite ambiguous and do not always appear adapted to the situation at hand.[4] The episode during which an official from the Castle tries to seduce a girl illustrates a situation analyzed by Kierkegaard in *Fear and Trembling:* the suspension of ethics by God himself, with a view to certain particular ends. The vexing contradictions which K. discovers among the measures adopted by the officials again reminds us of how Kierkegaard describes the contradictions of the Bible: necessary to safeguard the freedom of the act of faith and thereby paradoxical proofs of the divine inspiration of the Scriptures. Lastly, the antagonism between the inn, where the Gentlemen from the Castle stay, and the Farm, where Barnabas' despised family lives, seems to me to correspond to the struggle among the established churches and the small groups of illuminated dissidents. The inn inspires the respect due to wealth and ancestral customs, but Barnabas, the reprobate, is ultimately the only one to obtain almost direct communication.

Uncertainties, delays in transmission, cruel failures of good will, disappointing successes due to chance or to the caprice of a generally incompetent official, morbid fatigue, false resignation, childish defiance—all derive from a single spiritual state: doubt. Not doubt as to the existence of God, once again, but doubt as to the reality of *gratuitous* forgiveness, of grace incarnated, fulfilled in history. And, of course, such doubt will always be inseparable from faith in the concrete aspect of a

[4] Kierkegaard has discussed this notion several times—that the Bible must be read as a letter addressed to us personally and not as a purely objective narrative.

Christian life. That cry of a father before Christ: "Lord, I believe; help thou mine unbelief" is the cry of living faith, always opposed by the sense of sight, by natural certainty. Indeed, it is so difficult to conceive of a living faith without doubt that we are tempted to consider doubt as a dialectical proof of faith. The extraordinary thing about Kafka is that he could have suffered so consciously, and detailed with such patient ferocity, the elements of uncertainty which in others indicate faith —when he himself did not have it. The Christian recognizes himself in this work, and at the same time he feels ill at ease within it; everything is clearly seen, and with what pitiless eyes for the illusions of routine or of morality, but everything is seen *from the viewpoint of vertigo* and not from that of accepted love. The "leap" Kierkegaard speaks of is constantly imagined, but never taken. There is no *fait accompli:* there has been no incarnation. There remains an ironic and exhausted clearsightedness; and perhaps a last hope of escaping despite God's absence; a last hope of making a life for oneself by dint of application, of honesty in small efforts—against a huge background of absurdity.

*III   "K." between Kierkegaard's madness and Goethe's wisdom*

It would seem that *The Castle,* a posthumous novel, must end with K.'s failure, this hero dying of exhaustion without having achieved anything certain. "Round his deathbed, the villagers were to assemble, and from the Castle itself word was to come that though K.'s legal claim to live in the village was not valid, yet, taking certain auxiliary circumstances into account, he was to be permitted to live and work there." Max Brod, who reports this conclusion, projected by his friend, chooses to see in it an echo of these lines from the Second Part of *Faust:*

*Wer immer strebend sich bemüht*
*Den können wir erlösen.*

(Who strives forever onward,
Him can we save.)

And Kafka's biography confirms this interpretation.

Is it not curiously moving that a mind so lucid and scrupulous can have developed, or rather oscillated, in all consciousness, from Kierkegaard to Goethe? Do not these two names designate the poles of the most dizzying spiritual tension it has been given a Western man to experience? Yes, Kiekegaard and Goethe are, in my eyes, the most inspired personifications of an ethic based on pure transcendence and an ethic based on pure immanence. They exclude each other with violence, and even with disgust. Kierkegaard never had sarcasms enough for the solemn wisdom of the Weimar Councilor, and the latter would not have failed to condemn the "madness" and "absurdity" of the Dane in the name of the vital equilibrium so passionately conquered by Faust.

That is why it is crucial for me to locate Kafka's work

in relation to the two masters whom he had chosen, and whom he did not cease to cultivate, it seems, simultaneously.

To say that the sense of divine transcendence is, in Kafka, almost physical is to risk a contradiction in terms. Transcendence in itself and by definition escapes all natural meaning, rational as well as physical. But, provided the mind has received some presentiment of it, some revelation, however furtive and ambiguous, however veiled, however anonymous or pseudonymous, then a new anguish is born. Of course, the world of bodies, feelings, and ideas remains the only world perceptible to our various faculties, remains the only world in which we have to live. But, although nothing is changed in its appearances, everything in the world assumes precisely the look of appearances; everywhere the aspect of doubt is insinuated. This is the faint draft of air which the creature of *The Burrow* believes it hears whistling through the perpetually reopened cracks of its subterranean dwelling. Every object, every thought, and every encounter now seem to reveal some error, some subtle but essential defect, some irreducible and irritating sophism. Or might it be that everything signifies and supposes something else? Yet it is impossible to know what; no one has pierced the veil, and the intercepted messages are not clear. Transcendence, in our life, can be manifested only in a negative form: in anguish, in the feeling of a strange lack of ultimate meaning. And, in effect, the Absurd of which Kierkegaard spoke, in full

knowledge of the revealed cause—sin—is in Kafka only
a vague sentiment, but at the same time an ineluctable
one. The exactitude of the soberest and, let us even say,
of the most skeptical vision multiplies in everyday life the
opportunities to catch the incongruous, the lack of
satisfactory meaning, the necessity "for something else,"
whose nature remains unimaginable.

This sentiment of metaphysical anguish—but experienced negatively, in the concrete details of defective
life—is strictly intolerable. Or, rather, it would be
tolerable only for the man who had grasped, even if
only once, the promise of his deliverance. In fact, it is
only the Christians who acknowledge the sin of the
world, for it is their faith which reveals it at the very
moment it reveals forgiveness. According to the image
of Theresa of Avila, often reinvented by the great
spiritual writers, it is the ray of light passing through
the penumbra which reveals the millions of specks of
dust suspended in the air we believed pure. Now Kafka's
singular vision can discern all these specks of dust, but
without the ray of light. A unique and almost unthink-
able case, and yet magnificently attested to by an art in
which everything signifies that the supreme signification
remains an enigma! The kind of methodical frenzy—
somehow made infinitely deliberate by a fraternal pity—
which inspires this experience might lead us to suspect
Kafka of a *cathartic* intention, a deliverance by excess.
If he makes man's situation as he sees it so physically
unendurable, is it not to provoke him to a decision that
is equivalent to an act of faith?

If this were the case, it would be wise to observe that the very *données* of the conflict would predetermine its solution. The effort to surmount transcendental anguish by purely human means could not conclude other than in the ethic of immanence, which is that of the Second Part of *Faust*. The hero of *The Trial*, Joseph K., had found himself condemned by justice, lacking a lawyer from on high. In *The Castle*, K. will resign himself to live, in spite of everything, by his efforts. Not that he denies the existence of grace. But he repeats with the sages—he, the madman—*quae super nos, nihil ad nos,* and he draws from it the practical consequences. He entrenches himself in "harsh reality." He tries to acquire there sufficient merits not in order to enter the Kingdom of Heaven, but simply not to be rejected from the common human condition. He will imitate the Philistines in all their gestures, aware of recovering by this effort a *droit de cité*, which for the others is unquestioned. A Kierkegaardian anguish at its source, but which, failing to conclude in an *Allelujah!*, falls back upon an *Et allons!* A Goethean solution in its apparent goals, but against a background of hostile absurdity, and not of confidence in nature.

The knight of faith, in Kierkegaard, continually performed the "leap" into the absolute, or into the absurd, but performed it in such a way that he landed with both feet on the ground and could henceforth act and advance as if nothing had happened. He had "the look of a tax collector," and he was a witness to faith, in the name of absurdity accepted, who henceforth moved freely in love. But if K.[5] resigns himself to reality, it is in the name of an absurd which he flees, in the name of the fear of an inaccessible God Who laughs at our lucidity, not to mention our tragi-comic efforts to seduce or dupe him.

The knight of faith, too, once again on terra firma, could accept the morality lesson of the Second Part of *Faust*, as an ethic of the Incarnation, as a work expressing faith in the temporary order of the fallen world, as a way of renouncing knowing God other than by obeying the actual demands of His love. But K.'s example suggests another function of the Goethean wisdom. This morality can no doubt be adopted, in its form, by a believer; but it may also remain without content of hope or faith, and without any other purpose than a terrestrial one. A school of the person, it can also become a simple school of personalities. . .whence the suspicion in which many Christians hold Faust's sober activism. Instead of seeing in it a virile modesty, and a refusal of the *speculatio maiestatis*, they discern the Promethean temptation of a world organized without God, of an autarchy of immanence.

But is not such an ambiguity ultimately the result of any morality, of any wisdom, even one of Christian inspiration? And may not the Kierkegaardian *person*,

---

[5] K. and not Kafka. It would not be just to assimilate the author's inner experience to that which he causes his hero to undergo. I am certain that ultimately Kafka remains much closer to Kierkegaard than to Goethe.

based on pure transcendence, become at any moment just what it seems: a respectable personality, subject to immanence alone, the knight of faith looks like a tax collector; who can swear that he is, in fact, anything more than a tax collector?[6] We are here in a realm where we cannot imagine an unambiguous certitude. For this is the domain of faith. And faith alone—which is not verifiable—can verify the work done in its name. All we can say comes down to saying *in the name of what* we act, despite the "absurdity" of our action or its rational appearance. The evidence by word of mouth, of which Saint Paul speaks, the allegation of final motives —such is the only human criterion that would authorize us to distinguish in Goethe, in Kierkegaard, and in Kafka the possible role of faith. And, of course, I have confronted them in these pages only by the means of their expressions: where their experiences become comparable either because they are opposed term for term or their formulas intersect. But we must not forget that Kafka never explained himself, and that he died without having been able to provide the equivalent of Goethe's *Conversations* or of Kierkegaard's opusculum on his activity as an author.

If then we are sometimes tempted to infer from these three magnificent *oeuvres* some judgment of value as to the intimate experience which they betoken or *betray*,

[6] And I am not even discussing the Philistine, incapable of suspecting that his biped morality may be a renunciation of Icarus' flight, such folly never having *tempted* him in the slightest.

Kafka's example is the most likely to remind us of the apostolic admonition: "The Lord knows His own." Quite differently from the way we know them; differently, even, from the way they have known themselves.
—*1939*

# Two

# Freedom

**and Fatum**

# Luther and
# the Liberty of the Person

To say that Luther is unknown in France would be an exaggeration, but in a direction contrary to what one might suppose. For we are worse than ignorant of Luther, and not even contemptuous of him; we claim, without ever having read him, to know who he was, who he is. Some of us have glanced through the *Table Talk*, presented to the French public as a capital work; such readers are amazed to find so little theological substance and so many often crude jokes, platitudes, and contradictions. Was it of such stuff that the Reformation was made? Others, less demanding, do not hesitate to assert that Luther was a demagogue, exploiting the German race's eternal resentment of Roman civilization. Instead of referring certain of Luther's defects to his original Germanism, everything that is offensive in today's Germany is referred to Lutheranism, as if Luther had created Germanism. As if he were the ancestor not of Niemöller, a Christian and a Lutheran, but of Hitler, a Catholic-born pagan. As for the average opinion of Luther, I suspect that the following remark affords a fair notion: "After all, what was Luther? A monk who wanted to get married. . . ."

The current ignorance or contempt of Luther, combined with the various calumnies amassed by amateur biographers, and the effect of Catholic polemics (Denifle, Maritain, Grisar), plunge the French public into a state of serious inferiority on the level of general culture. For to be ignorant or contemptuous of Luther is to be ignorant or contemptuous of one of the two or three decisive moments of the Western tradition, is to prevent any understanding of the great, millennial debate, the great spiritual tension from which Europe has drawn her creative dynamism—a tension in which the argument of free will, opposing Erasmus to Luther, permits us to reach a symbolic definition of the poles: "pure" thought and "engaged" thought, or, again, the attitude of a spectator and the attitude of a witness. This is an opposition which, on the theological level or, better still, in the totality of being, comes down to that of a Christianity mitigated by human respect and an absolute Christianity, which is readily characterized as "inhuman" because it attributes everything to God.

## "De Servo Arbitrio"

When, in 1537, it was suggested that Luther publish his complete works, the Reformer replied: "I acknowledge none of my books as sufficient, except perhaps the *Servo Arbitrio* and the *Catechism*."

Hence, with the *Servo Arbitrio,* by the author's own admission, we are at the heart of the Reformation and its dogmatic effort. But we thereby approach the most arduous problem posed by the autonomy of the person: the problem of the liberty of the person and of the ultimate basis of his responsibility. For the person, in the life of the individual, is simultaneously the liberating element—with regard to the natural *données*—and the ordering element—with regard to the vocation. In other words, the liberty of the person is not an attribute of the individual as such, but is attributed to him by a gratuitous summons of the Spirit. If the natural man is not free to accede to liberty, this freedom can be *given* him by the vocative power of God.[1] Such is the fundamental thesis of the *De Servo Arbitrio,* written in 1525 to refute the *Diatribe seu collatio de libero arbitrio,* published by Erasmus the preceding year.

One first assumes the work to be a pamphlet, though its material volume is quite burdensome for the genre. But it is soon apparent that the argument with Erasmus and his (often personified) *Diatribe* is in fact only the pretext for a reflection of broader scope, for testimony that transcends all disputation. Swept on by his customary passion, aroused (rather than "disarmed," as he says in the first pages) by the methods of the humanist and skeptic Erasmus boasts of being, Luther succeeds step by step in reapprehending and powerfully restating all the basic assertions of the Reformation: justification by

[1] The paradox that constituted the subject of the brief treatise *De libertate christiana* (1520) expresses the dialectic no longer of the Christian individual but of the Christian *person:* "The Christian is a free master over all things, and is subject to no one. The Christian is in all things a servant, and depends on everyone." The French edition of this little work, translated by the Abbé Christiani, adds an entertaining note at this point: "From the very first lines, Luther betrays the systematic spirit by which the entire work is inspired, in the entirely artificial and arbitrary play of antithesis." The author forgets that Luther has merely paraphrased I Corinthians, IX, 19 at cant: "For though I be free from all *men,* yet have I made myself servant unto all . . ." The "arbitrary and artificial antithesis," then, is Saint Paul's.

faith, which is a gratuitous gift and the work of God alone; opposition of this Divine Justice to the justice of men and their works; opposition of Grace to nature, according to the Apostle's terms; opposition of the living Word to the codified tradition; sense of the total decision between an absolute yes and an absolute no, and refusal of any middle term, any more-or-less rational mediation between the contradictory realms of the God of faith and of the Prince of this world; necessity of bearing faithful witness, attested to by the Spirit and the Bible, and constituting the true "action" of man "in the hands of God."

Such are the themes with which this work deals. If they are not treated formally, it is because they do not constitute a system, in the philosophical sense of the word, but inevitably imply each other and cannot be handled better than in the unique and perpetual question which every page of the Bible raises. They refer everything to a reality of which they are only the reflections variously refracted by our words. They refer everything to Christ's question: "Believe ye that I am able to do this?" If you believe this, if you have received the faith, there is nothing "difficult" in Luther's assertions nor in his joyous negation of free will. His violent blows shake only the old Adam, the man we must all slough off.

But there is almost every reason why the great Pauline theses of the Reformation should not be accepted (or even known!) by our contemporaries, even when they are Christians. It would take a great deal, almost everything, for the arguments of an Erasmus to seem to us so many sophisms. Not only do all the humanists—from Marxists to old liberals—applaud them openly, but even among Christians these arguments are reinvented, admitted, sometimes even preached. Secular moralizing has no monopoly on them: every Catholic must, if he is logical, make them his own, since he believes in the merit of works; and every Protestant who still believes that Calvin and Luther have served their turn—and what shall we say of Paul, so much older still!—all who regard predestination as an immoral or superseded doctrine; those who translate: "Peace on earth, good will toward men" as "Peace on earth to men of good will"—all these agree, in fact, with Erasmus and his army of "great doctors of all ages" in championing religious free will, that is, *man's power to contribute to his salvation by his efforts and his moral works.*

What will they find, then, in this treatise of Luther's? A polemical verve that may tickle a taste for the picturesque; the inspired *élan,* the partisan violence of a grave, truly "heavy" certitude, of a sober and stubborn dialectic which goes straight to the decisive point, considers objections honestly, gives the adverse thesis all its opportunities, though not without irony, and lastly is able to confer upon its choice the force and simplicity of recognition of the facts. From a purely esthetic point of view, these qualities are rare enough, and in Luther flagrant enough, for a reader who refuses the essential to be nonetheless attracted and won over by the style, the tone of the work. (We know only too well, we moderns, how to separate form from content; to admire one when we condemn the other, and vice versa.)

But once we acknowledge this mastery, which after all we might expect from the leader of a great movement (as today's jargon would say), everything in our treatise is likely to shock the unbelieving reader or the reader who does not share the faith of Paul and the Apostles. First of all, the scholastic language, which is not at all Lutheran, but which Luther is obliged to use in order to clarify and suppress the pseudo-problems in which the *Diatribe* sought to ensnare him.[2] Then, this utter rejection, or better, this calm neglect of any kind of psychological consideration—such a man is too vital to psychologize, too *engaged* in reality to take seriously its reflections in the spectator's consciousness—which will, of course, bring charges of dogmatism down upon his head. Here everything occurs "within" Christianity, "within" the church. Autonomous, secular humanism is simply denied as an absurdity, a contradiction in terms. It is to Erasmus as *theologian* that Luther is concerned to reply; and it is even the harshest irony—though an involuntary one, I presume—with which he could, in this case, overwhelm him.

We cannot emphasize this characteristic too strongly: It is always as a theologian, as a faithful doctor of the church, as a responsible preacher, not as a philosopher or a metaphysician, that Luther denies free will. This should and must suffice to refute the modern objection, the utterly anachronistic though inevitable objection that Luther is a "determinist." But theological seriousness is something too rare and, for many, too difficult to grasp

[2] Luther warns on each occasion: "Conditional necessity and absolute necessity, as others call them," and this *others* designates "the Sophists," that is, the Scholastics.

for this objection to be dispelled by a simple reminder of the order in which this treatise was conceived.

I shall therefore attempt to sketch, at least, the dialogue of a "modern conscience" endowed with spiritual needs and a partisan of the Lutheran *servo arbitrio*. (We may suppose that such a dialogue takes place within the mind of a man who honestly seeks to believe.)

*Dialogue*

> "For God can do anything at any moment. That is the health of faith."—Kierkegaard

THE MODERN CONSCIENCE: According to Luther, we have no freedom, for in reality God has foreseen everything and nothing happens except according to His prevision. Luther poses not only the omnipotence, but the omniscience and the eternal prescience of God, Who cannot fail in His covenant and against Whom no obstacle is raised. What then becomes of our effort? It no longer serves any purpose. We shall do no more. We refuse to play, if the winner has been chosen in advance by a referee who does not keep track of our exploits!

A LUTHERAN: But do you at least know the true rules of the game? Who has led you to believe that your life was a game to be played between yourself and the world, for instance, or between the individual and fortune, that pagan idol?

MC: I need to believe this in order to act.

L: But what is *to act*? Is it really you who acts? Or are you not *acted* upon by powerful social, historical, and economic forces? Is not all your science precisely concerned with discovering them? Or even with inventing them?

MC: Certainly, but my dignity consists in struggling against such forces—once I have recognized them—in affirming myself in my autonomy by an act that creates my freedom, by an act of revolt, if need be!

L: Then you believe you possess such a power?

MC: It is enough to seek to affirm it.

L: That will do as a working hypothesis. Myself, I believe that God knows the end, the whole, the absolute value of our past, present, and future actions, for they are in time; God in eternity, which is before time, in time, and after time. In God's eyes, then, "all is consummated"— since the death of Christ on the cross, not only foreseen but fulfilled.

MC: If that were true, I should still prefer to deny this God, Who claims to see beyond the term of my actions—which, we must admit, makes them completely absurd and ultimately futile—for I feel, in spite of everything, that I perform them freely, and you have just told me that they are foreseen! And foreseen by an eternal God, Who thereby plays with me shamefully! So it comes down to a choice: God or Me. I say: Me. Even if I have to kill God, as Nietzsche claimed he had done.

L: How can time kill eternity? How can the flesh kill the Spirit? It can kill only its own false notions. . . . Nietzsche has seen this clearly: It is only the "moral God" Who is susceptible of refutation. But you assert that if God foresees everything, you are then dispensed from acting and it is no longer worth making any effort. Perhaps you are reasoning badly. What if your effort were also foreseen? *Could you* not make it? And what if you decided: "I am, therefore God does not exist!"[3]—what assurance do you have that this act of revolt escapes the eternal prevision? What assurance do you have that in speaking these words you are not speaking God's eternal decree upon yourself, casting yourself into nothingness, so that God, truly, no longer exists *for you?* There is a double predestination: one to salvation, the other to damnation. To be damned—would you not that be, in fact, to be fettered to time without end and to refuse the eternity which delivers us from time?

MC: But time is alive and filled with novelty, with creation! Your motionless eternity is the very image of death.

L: What do we know of eternity? Philosophers and reason can conceive it only as dead. But the Bible tells us that it is Life, and our present life is only a death in its eyes. What proves that eternity is motionless, static? What suggests that it is not, on the contrary, the source of every act and of all creation, a total and perpetual invention, a permanent present, precisely what changes something in the calculable process of time, when it touches it within the *instant* (within the "moment" of time, as Paul says)? What assurance do you have that our reason, attached as it is to our flesh, to our time, in which it has been constituted, is capable of conceiving this paradox or this scandal of an eternity that is *only* present? This is a mystery deeper than our life, and reason is only a secondary element of our life. This is a mystery which the believer realizes and experiences at the moment

[3] Like the anarchist Bakunin.

of prayer alone. "Ask, and it shall be given you," says the *same* God Who predestined us! When the believer, who knows that God has foreseen all and forever, addresses to God, in the name of his covenant, a specific and urgent prayer, does he not experience this paradox and this mystery: To believe that "the Eternal is living," to believe that His will—which has foreseen all—can also change all in an instant, to the eyes of man, without anything being changed in what God has decided, decides, or shall decide? For the Eternal knows no tense, is not bound, like us, to succession. But on the contrary, our various tenses and successions proceed from the Eternal and are bound to Him: we come from Him; we return to Him; He is in us when the Spirit speaks the Word in our hearts. What strange illusion would make us believe that a decision of the Eternal is a decision *in the past!* When it is the Eternal alone Who defines our present! Are not our philosophical objections and our fear of "fatalism" most often based on this error of the crudest sort? . . .[4]

MC: We can also deny eternity, and assert that only our time exists. In that case, you have proved nothing.

L: One never proves anything that is essential, but one accepts or refuses it by virtue of a pure decision. Argument can lead us only to the threshold of this decision. And we shall not have debated in vain if we have been able to reveal the alternative of free will, as

[4] See the philosophical objections of Jules Lequier against the prescience of God. All are based on this notion: that an eternal decision of God's is a decision which has been taken *before* our acts—long before—"from all eternity" as the saying goes.

it is posed in the extreme terms where it assumes its true
reality: either the Eternal commands—or I. There are
no intellectual difficulties here. There is only the resistance of the old Adam and the always moral, even pious
excuses our revolt invokes. . . .

## Radical Reality of the Problem

In the Church, once we accept the Credo and its basis,
which is the Word spoken within us by the Spirit and
attested by Scripture—and this Word is Christ himself
—it seems to me that Luther's opinion is not susceptible
to serious objections. And the *purely biblical* demonstration of the *De Servo Arbitrio,* despite a few exegetical
details open to question, suffices to establish for the
Christian the truth of a paradox which Luther has not
invented but which is at the very heart of the Gospels.
The Apostle Paul formulated it in advance of any
ecclesiastical tradition; and all the Fathers and all the
ages Erasmus appeals to will change nothing about it:
". . . *work* out your own salvation with fear and trembling.
*For* it is God which worketh in you both to will and to
do . . ." (Phil. II, 12–13) It is *because* God does all,
that we must act according to His command. It is because
God foresees all, that we have freedom in Him and in
Him alone. But this is evident only to the man who dares
proceed to the extremes of self-knowledge and the knowledge of faith, for faith alone reveals the radical nature
of sin. Luther insists on this evangelical extremism, which
the Sophists were only too inclined to correct and to

humanize, at the risk of "emptying the Cross." So long
as one has not envisaged the doctrine of pure grace in to
its ultimate seriousness, one may assert that man possesses at least "some light free will"[5] in the matter of
salvation. But the fact that Christ had to *die* in order to
save us—and death is an extreme act, not a flattering
and humanist mediation—reveals that we have no possible freedom, except in the grace God accords us. All
of Luther's disputation focuses on the moment of the
decision, and neglects the middle terms in which Erasmus
indulged himself. The problem of salvation is a problem
of life or death. Now this problem is the only one at stake
for the faithful theologian. And everything is clear when
we have understood that Luther is not denying our
psychological faculty to will but only denying that this
faculty can *suffice* to obtain salvation for us, itself being
subject to evil. All the rest is psychology, literature, and
scholasticism.[6]

It remains true, nonetheless, that in the eyes of rea-

[5] *Modiculum et minimum!* writes Erasmus.

[6] Or else obscurantism. One distinguished French professor did
not hesitate to qualify Lutheran Christianity as the "religion of
the servile will." (He based his arguments for doing so upon
Grisar.) One might as well say that Luther's religion was the religion of sin! Or that the *Christian* liberty Luther preaches is to
be identified with the rationalist and entirely modern notion of
contingence, which Luther nowhere envisages. The same author
commits the unforgivable error of relating the *Servo Arbitrio* to
determinism—only in order to attack the "Germanism" that
destroys all freedom! This kind of abuse is too frequent for me
to be able to pass it over in silence. (I was referring to Monsieur
Jacques Chevalier, who had become a minister of the Vichy
government.—1944 note)

son—that madwoman, that whore, as Luther keeps calling her—what we are here calling a paradox remains a pure and simple absurdity. "To the reason, it seems cruel, unjust and intolerable to affirm that God damns whom He will—to the scorn of so many great men of all ages. And who would not be scandalized?" Thus speaks Luther himself, and it is the natural man in him who makes this complaint. But he adds: "I must confess that this thought has wounded me deeply and even to despair, so that I desired not to have been born, *before I had acknowledged how salutary was this despair and how near to grace*." For indeed: "It is the highest degree of faith to believe that this God is clement, Who saves so few men and damns so great a number; and that this God is just, Whose will renders us necessarily damnable . . . But then! If we managed to comprehend by reason in what manner God is merciful and just, *what need would we have of faith?* . . . It would be a stupid God who revealed to men (in Christ) a justice which they already knew, or whose innate spark they would have in themselves." Here it is faith alone, gift of grace, which speaks. In the conflict between this revelation and the natural resistances—a victorious conflict for faith—abide the strictly Lutheran tension and the sense of vocation. I see Luther's immeasurable greatness in this will to reduce himself to *absurdity* in the eyes of the man who refuses his decision.

But, then, we may ask if those who refuse Christianity really escape the difficulty; if, on the contrary, they do not encounter it on a level where it remains insoluble. Erasmus was still a Catholic; his measured humanism prevented him from seeing the real tragedy of the debate. But the greatest adversary of Christianity in modern times, Nietzsche, arrives at a dilemma which seems to me to correspond, term for term, to the one which both Luther and Paul propose to our faith. This is because Nietzsche, like Luther, has proceeded to man's extreme limits, to the ultimate questions which our thought can envisage. In order to escape the nihilism in which he founders, once "God is dead" or once he has "killed" Him, Nietzsche conceives the Eternal Return. And since this Eternal Return seems to exclude all human freedom, he begins preaching *amor fati,* the voluntary and joyous adherence to ineluctable fatality. It is in this desire to acknowledge our total irresponsibility that he believes he will find and regain the supreme dignity of man without God.

The astonishing similarity of the Lutheran paradox and the Nietzschean one cannot be reduced to some unconscious influence, still less to a coincidence. The truth is, the same problem is at stake—the only problem, once one comes to a radical test of life. To God's "thou shalt," Nietzsche opposed the "I would" of the divinized man. Then he opposed the existence of God by his own existence. But the fundamental difficulty raised by the relations of our will and sovereign eternity remains intact. The difference is that Nietzsche proposes that we adore a mute Destiny, while Luther adores a Providence Whose living Word has been incarnated, reversing the Law's *imperative*—which condemns us, for we are subject— into a *power* to love, which liberates us and which is the content of Grace: "Emmanuel! God with us!"

# John Calvin:
# An "Engaged" Writer

If we agree with the manifesto serving as an introduction
to the revived *Nouvelle Revue Française* of 1953 that
"the writer, insofar as he concerns himself with the
vicissitudes of his times and attempts to involve himself
in them—to direct them, why not?—does not perform
precisely the writer's task," then Calvin is not a writer.
He has created a style and a vocabulary, and the language
of ideas in France, and Bossuet concedes him "the glory
of having written as well as any man of his age," but this
was not in order to produce literature; it was to teach
religious truths in the vicissitudes of his times, and to
direct men to their goal of salvation. He wrote only to
make Scripture better understood; spoke only to gain a
better hearing for the Word. The idea of awakening
interest by turns of phrase or unexpected adjectives, by
obscure or brilliant formulations, a tone of grandeur or
of trivial naturalness, of despair or exquisite discretion,
any *tone* at all—the very idea of being original—did not
occur to him for a second. One does not play with words
when one is "Minister of the Word," *minister verbi
divini*.

Whatever the textbooks say, I do not see that Calvin
has had the slightest ascertainable "influence" on French
literature, although the virtues of clarity, proportion,
propriety in terms and rigor in their articulation, which
are often called Cartesian, were first illustrated in our
language by his writings—an historical fact, but not a

matter of continuous presence. What is meant in our times by "literature," in the circles where it is created and cultivated for its own sake, is defined precisely as something in which Calvin would not find his place and, thereby, no longer plays any part.

On the other hand, one of the prevailing traditions of French thought, the one that regards the writer as a man charged with a normative mission to create general values in the City—this "classical" or social attitude of the mind, which in my earlier works I attempted to describe by the term "engagement," a term that seems to have been somewhat abused—doubtless originates with Calvin, and has never yet equaled its model.

Calvin is not gracious, moreover, as we know. Lean and melancholy, like Charles the Fifth—while Luther is as fat as Thomas Aquinas, and more jovial—he beguiles us only by the extremes of an inflexible inner discipline. Nothing is less dry, moreover, or livelier than his prose. But let us leave questions of taste aside. What is of significance to me here is the *effectiveness* of a work written and thought entirely within absolute submission to a cause that transcends the author.

A man pursued by his vocation.

His father intended him to study law, because it enriched those who followed it, he tells us. "God however turned me from that path . . . Having thus received some taste and knowledge of the true piety, I was forthwith inflamed with so great a desire to grow in this wisdom, that though I did not leave off my other studies, I nonetheless employed myself upon them less diligently. Yet I was quite amazed that before the year was out, all those who had some desire of pure doctrine turned to me to learn of it, though I had only commenced it myself. Being, moreover, of a somewhat timid and rude nature, I have always loved repose and tranquillity, and I began to seek for some place of retirement and the means of turning away from men. But so far was I from achieving my desire that, on the contrary, all retreats and places of obscurity were even as public schools to me. In short, though I had always this goal of living in private, without being known, God has so brought me forward and turned me about by various changes that He has never left me at rest in any place until, despite my nature, He has brought me forth in the light and called me into play, as it is said."

The story reaches a climax in 1535, a crucial year, when, while three great translations of the Bible appear (Luther's in Germany, Tyndale's in England, Robert Olivétan's in Switzerland), François I signs a totalitarian decree forbidding the printing of any book at all on pain of death. Calvin, fleeing from city to city, reaches Basel, intending to live there in concealment and obscurity. But the news from France, where his friends are being burned so that they can be calumniated more readily, obliges him to take up the defense of the "holy martyrs," lest, he says, by holding his peace he show himself to be cowardly and disloyal. It is thus that he composes in Latin, between March and August, the 520 pages of his first *Institutes of the Christian Religion,* then, in French, the Prefatory Epistle to the King of France. He is twenty-five years old. In a few months he has produced—"in memorable, celestial lucubrations," the humanist Ramus will write—one of the rare books that have changed the course of our Western history. And again he flees before the uproar which this "*petit livret*," as he calls it, makes in the world; he passes through Geneva, intending to remain only one night. But here, "Maître Guillaume Farel retained me, not so much by counsel and exhortation as by a dreadful adjuration, as if God had from on high stretched out His hand to keep me." This brings an end to the peace of his studies, condemned by Farel's outcries. However, he accepts only an office as Doctor, and begins to "train" the Church within his disciplines. Soon, a sedition drives him away. Can he regard himself as "at liberty and absolved of his vocation"? Already Bucer demands his presence at Strasbourg, "using a similar remonstrance to that which Farel had invoked erstwhile." Calvin becomes the pastor of the first reformed church, and provides it with a liturgy, which he versifies so that it may be sung more readily. Three years pass and his thought ripens, but now Geneva recalls him. "Against my desire and affection, I was persuaded of the necessity to return to my first charge . . . which I did with sadness, tears, great solicitude and distress. . . . Now, if I desired to recite the diverse combats by which the Lord has tried me since that time, and by what ordeals He has examined me, it would be a long history indeed." Like King David molested by wars and grieving among his people over the malice of the disloyal, "I have been so beset that it is with great difficulty that I have been able to be at peace even a short time without having to sustain some new dispute, either from those without, or from those within."

Thus, from summons to summons, Jean Chauvin, the frail Picard, becomes John Calvin, the name of his *persona* in history.

To follow one's vocation, contrary to what is generally believed, is not to follow one's inclination (even uphill), but to be swept in spite of oneself toward goals and into an action to which nothing whatever inclines us. *I am the man least suited for this!* groans the individual, when an unknown force, wrenching him from himself, flings him upon his *persona*. And Calvin: "God turned me from that path . . ." His effectiveness is born of this surrender, of this condign defeat unremittingly inflicted upon the natural individual by what is not him, but which comes to *summon* him and creates him forever.

All the virtues of his style derive from this tension established by his vocation, as also his defects, according to the taste of the day. He is less attractive than imperious, yet less imperious than coercive by a bitter logic colored by proverbs, crude fables, and countless quotations from the Bible restored to their most abrupt and prosaic novelty. His "baroque" is that of the common-sense and everyday language of his time; we mistakenly regard as picturesque turns of speech which sought merely to be clear and convincing for his contemporaries. To the eloquent rhetoric—mannerist *à la* Michelangelo, sometimes even *à la* Greco—of the *Epistle* to François I, let us oppose the urgent and familiar movement of the daily *Sermons* he preached in the Cathédral de Saint-Pierre. Nothing is closer to improvised speech; nothing is more varied in its rhythms; and yet nothing is more loftily monotonous in its prevailing thought: to God alone everything is due, and from Him alone everything comes. The sentences are often long, but of steady progress, leading toward a goal so strongly conceived that no frivolous doubt could ever even momentarily deter the mind that composed them. This is the language of a leader—but a spiritual one—speaking in a besieged city, whether Geneva, where he kept watch on the ramparts, or the church, harassed by persecution, or the weak heart of man, exposed to the world's attacks. He must "press" his audience, instruct it "to salvation," "comfort" it in the paternal love of a God-King tremendously exalted above the powerful of the earth, yet jealous of His rights and the interests of "His" people. This is a language divested of all churchly unction, inspired solely by the desire to educate the people and their princes. A language, finally, of a man who knows he is being heard not only by the Genevans but by an entire European elite, gathered before him at the foot of the pulpit, and whose concrete circumstances he knows well—whence the absence of doubt and playfulness, of the gratuitous and the ornamental, whence the nakedness of the words, but also their power of contagion.

The minister of the Word has made a world.

He is even the only writer whose doctrines have produced in the West a civic and social ethic; a new type of political relations; and, lastly, forms of government which have left a decisive mark on England and her dominions, Holland and Switzerland, Hungary for a time, Huguenot France, finally all of North America—and this comprises half the West. I seek in vain the mind comparable to his for scope and duration of an action of this order in history. I rule out Rousseau, his disciple but also his perfect antithesis; who still believes in the goodness of the natural man? I rule out Machiavelli, that great, misunderstood figure. I rule out Nietzsche. I see only Marx, and yet . . . An international empire claims its descent from his work, or at least from his name; yet is it justified in doing so? Of course, we may assert that the United States would be as severely judged by Calvin as Russia is by Marx. But Marxism, despite a doctrine of history to all intents and purposes predestinational, and almost as paradoxical as that of the Fathers of the Reformation, has never been able to create an ethic, nor even a formula of equilibrium, among nations or princes, still less between the citizen and the state.

Calvin was not a democrat, but he has stirred up the leaders who taught future ages that there is no concrete freedom which is not, in return, responsible before God and in the City, and that the title of citizen is less a right than a duty. The Western democracies who have refused to pay this price have died because of it, or are worth little more than if they were dead.

The synodal regime of the Reformed churches prefigures a secular government by elected representatives. The principle of the right to revolt, denied to individuals but entrusted as a duty to constituted groups when the state exceeds its functions, has protected the Calvinist peoples not only against anarchy but also against its most brutal antidotes. On the map of the modern West, compare Calvin's sphere of influence and that of the totalitarian dictatorships; they nowhere overlap. Finally, far from having established theocracy in Geneva, as common ignorance repeats, Calvin created the model of a church drawn up to confront the state and determined to keep it within the limits of its just *power,* that church itself asking none, since it holds *authority,* which is of the spirit.

Are we, then, to enlist Calvin in the ranks of freedom? Yes, insofar as only by virtue of his vocation was he the incarnation of authority; and insofar, too, as this driven man is accountable for the history of the freest states, because he did not believe in history deified but because he appealed to its Judge.

# Three

# Sincerity

**and Authenticity**

# The Journals
# of André Gide

## i

It would be disingenuous, even maladroit, not to admit the uncertainty in which such a book as the *Journals* involves the judgment. Gide has often repeated: *Judge not!* that he has ended by making himself "inestimable." How can we take a position in dealing with a man who constantly challenges any bias, and first of all with regard to himself? It is easy enough to renounce identifying him with one or another of the figures he reveals in the course of the *Journals;* but the critic's dilemma begins after this first trap has been avoided. It derives from the difficulty he has in discovering the inner hierarchy which would reveal, in this complex individual, the true person. Particularly since certain details, certain allusions, and many silences suggest a secret drama, a vital nexus in which the cause of the strangest contradictions Gide endures or entertains must abide. (To the point of occasionally masking true windows out of excessive mistrust of a symmetry that might tempt one to linger.)

Lacking a "judgment" which these 1,300 pages are resolved to denounce in advance, let us confine ourselves to marginal notes, to a few impressionist reactions.

What seduces, what fascinates in these *Journals* is nothing that can be defined in isolation—style, subjects treated, rhythm, ideas, anecdotes—but rather the secretly significant complexity of the whole. In order to describe this involuntary harmony, I can only invoke the example of Goethe, no one of whose works or actions are so admirable as the vital landscape, with its overcast skies and its suns, its parks, its fallows, and its habitations. The Goethe-phenomenon, in space and time, is what would give a notion of the kind of interest one takes in reading *The Journals of André Gide*. It is likely that from an exclusively artistic point of view, this interest remains impure; our modern indiscretion looks behind forms and beneath them, sifting the ores of fragmentary confidences for a truth which concerted works may have avowed much more clearly. It is also likely that the journal is an inferior literary genre, for it is always too easily interesting. I can regard it, as a work of art, only as limited to the narrative of a crisis, and subject even then to a kind of unity that is necessarily lacking in the intermittent chronicle of an existence. Despite the more elaborated pages which Gide has occasionally grouped under special titles (*Feuillets, Numquid et tu, La Marche turque,* etc.), despite the almost constant perfection of style—all those water colors and genre paintings in which mastery triumphs, even in the trivial—we can foresee that the value of such a work will remain of an essentially biographical order.

But this raises the problem of the portrait's truth to life. Gide himself notes as early as 1924: "If my journal is published later on, I fear that it will give a rather false idea of me. I have not kept it during the long periods of equilibrium, health, and happiness; but instead during those periods of depression when I needed it to catch hold of myself, in which I show myself as whining, whimpering, pitiable."

"If my journal is published later on . . ." He saw to that himself. And yet, "to give a false idea of himself" is just what Gide had to avoid, more jealously than anyone else. Is it really to diminish this risk that he anticipates it— or to disconcert his judges—that he lays down all his arms in advance? But this would be a poor calculation. In the eyes of a wary reader, so much "naturalness" might still pass for a refined pose. I should rather imagine that Gide is fascinated by the obstacle he wishes to avoid. His horror of misunderstanding leads him to give the public 1,300 pages of explanations which threaten to aggravate the ambiguity. But then, this becomes exemplary. The Gidean effort to escape the deceptive stylizations of ready-made moralities and judgments is not only moving, it assumes the value of a crucial experiment on the limits of sincerity in general and of the *journal intime* in particular. The passion for being *completely* honest ends by altering the natural; but by its very excess, it makes us aware of the continual defects of every self-portrait. It gives us the means of adding our own retouches to it.

Sometimes the secret of a life is exhausted in the work: the journal preserves only the driest notations (Byron, Stendahl). Sometimes the work and journal are merely different ways of pursuing one and the same confidence. We no longer know if the journal is a marginal comment on the work or if the work is only a privileged moment of this journal. Then the true portrait of the author is no longer in the work nor in the journal, but in their mutual refraction. And, for instance, the things left unspoken in this compendium—Gide has indicated that serious lacunae mutilate the image he offers of himself[1]—may perhaps be expressed in *Les Cahiers d'André Walter,* and above all in *Strait Is the Gate,* that Jansenist and "Catharist" novel.

Other causes of error intervene, distorting the proportions of the self-portrait, if we confine ourselves to the *Journals* alone. "The most important things are those I frequently have not felt I should say—because they seemed too obvious to me." However sincere one wants to be in relating one's days, how can one help being tempted to write most of what is striking, what is bizarre, what, in fact, is exceptional? And how can one avoid yielding to the temptation of a formula, an epigram on some friend about whom it seems pointless to repeat each time that one is fond of him? Thus one paints oneself more ill-natured than in nature, so to speak. Gide has not spared himself here: "I am only a little boy amusing himself—combined with a Protestant minister who bores him." This kind of sally some will not hesitate, against him, to abuse.

Here is a remark that takes us far in the criticism of the genre: "I do not think there is much to be gained from those soul-searchings in which one always manages to discover bad motives for any action. One will even invent them for the satisfaction of appearing more perceptive to oneself, and on the other hand, one tends to neglect, for fear of overpraise, any component of natural goodness

[1] *Journals,* January 26, 1939.

or sociability or, to put it better: of amiability, or better still: of the desire to seem amiable. But by watching oneself too much, one ceases to live. Here scrutiny creates what it seeks. . . ." Yet in writing this, has Gide not yielded to the temptation he describes: the vicious circle of sincerity?

Either one is commonplace—in order to re-establish the everyday proportions—or else one consents to note only what is important, that is, what is striking on that particular day, and makes oneself too picturesque. On the whole, the journal requires a discipline even greater than that of the work: One must impose on it a regular rhythm without gaps, an automatic and monotonous relation of minor facts, exactly *locating* the appearance of such and such an exceptional thought or act. But would this not be to the detriment of any lyrical impulse, of any great style of life rising from the depths and sometimes simplifying, with a broad paraph of joy or rage, the meticulous meanders of a sterile veracity?

The journals of writers are always true, but their truth is indirect, and occasionally even negative. It is not so much the life that has been lived that is expressed in them but the desire to complete or compensate for what has not been lived. ("I needed it to catch hold of myself.") Real life often figures in a journal only as it figures in dreams. Compensations, suppressions, repetitions of an *acte manqué* . . . It is a matter of knowing whether real life is in what one does or in what one thinks of one's actions.

But here I in my turn succumb to the desire to point

out only the discrepancies, forgetting what is obvious: Gide's self-portrait is a good likeness *too*. We find him here *au naturel,* with all his curiosity, his admirable modesty and his moments of malice, his rhythmic sense of the language always so firmly articulated (a habit from reading aloud), his flashes of humor and his need to agree with his adversary[2]. . . We find him here a naturalist in Goethe's style, and a musician as Goethe, again, wanted to be a painter. We discover him, finally—and this seems to me new—constantly concerned with religious problems— but in a manner we must qualify.

Has it been remarked to what degree Gide's "anti-Christianity" is Christian in its determinations? I think we have too often let ourselves be deceived by his perpetual polemic against the convert-converters. We must realize that for him, the religious problem was raised in terms which, almost necessarily, escape the solicitude of a Catholic.

Gide was raised in a Calvinist milieu where religion seemed to be reduced to those two elements which Calvin regards as heretical: free enquiry and moralism. From the former Gide has retained his demand for truth "come what may." The letter doubtless accounts for his fundamental propensity to prefer to the letter of dogma the spirit which inspires and qualifies our everyday actions, however nonconformist. But each morality in turn has soon been transformed into a dogma, and Protestant

---

[2] A need so contagious, when you talk to him or write about him, that you must force yourself not to abandon the positions you hold, which are not exactly Gide's.

morality succumbs to this danger more than any other in periods of theological depression. Whence the resentment which many Protestants conceive toward that morality, having become indifferent and merely subject to the habits of a milieu. Quite justified in itself, this reaction distorts certain of Gide's judgments on the Reformation; he often confuses it, I believe, with the common and false image of an inhuman, almost Manichean Calvin.

The anti-confessional evangelism which Gide retains from this early Christian education has put him on his guard against certain deformations—the most frequent— of Christianity: contempt for nature and, on the other hand, the recourse to orthodoxy as to an insurance taken on the Holy Ghost at least as much as on doubt. (He quotes this remark of a Catholic to a Protestant pastor: "You believe, but we know!") This explains why Gide's central concern has been to divest his Christianity of all the "human—all too human" adjunctions of neo-Protestant moralism and Roman dogmatism. Whence his congenital horror of all religious legerdemain. In sum, his entire effort consists of stripping himself of just what certain Christians sought to "reveal" to him. The problem of conversion becomes for him the negative problem of the false conversion, or of the too-easy conversion.

"Catholicism is inadmissible. Protestantism is intolerable. And I feel profoundly Christian." Or again: "I am neither Protestant nor Catholic; I am quite simply a Christian." A characteristic of liberal Protestantism as it developed in the last century.

"I often said to Claudel: What keeps me from entering

the Church is not freethinking, but the Gospels." But is there not in Gide, at the source of this rejection of the visibility of *any* church (Reformed as much as Roman), an attachment to his own truth which is less evangelical than individualist, or even rationalist. Not that I should venture to criticize an insistence on honesty which sometimes suggests Kierkegaard. Gide refuses to appear more than he is, to affirm more than he believes. He describes X, "obliged to sit at the family prayers. His embarrassment. *The horror of the gesture that may exceed its sentiment . . .*" Kierkegaard, too, repeated: I am not a Christian. But this was out of a desire to save a pure conception of the faith, of which he did not consider himself worthy, and which he thereby confessed. Gide seems chiefly concerned with his complex and reticent nature. Now every nature, irremediably, experiences itself as complex and reticent. And the act of faith will always consist in transcending the natural doubt, in confessing what neither flesh nor blood by themselves may confess. Then alone can be posed in clear terms the problem of the visible church, of obedience to an orthodoxy which does not claim to engross the Gospels but on the contrary to direct itself according to them. "Protestant orthodoxy," Gide writes, "for me these words have no meaning. I recognize no authority; and if I were to recognize one, it would be that of the Church" (in other words, of Rome). What then! For a Protestant, this dilemma is as shocking as the dilemma between anarchy and totalitarianism would be for an Englishman or a Scandinavian. To identify authority with Roman Catholicism is, moveover, one of the

most commonplace errors, in France particularly, and
even among certain Protestants separated from the life of
their church. All that I feel entitled to say here is that
the Reformation rejected the claims of the Pope of Rome
not out of disgust for authority as such but *on the contrary*
out of great fidelity to the authority of the Gospels, unique
and sufficient basis of the only liberating orthodoxy.


## ii

From the above, let us isolate and juxtapose these three
observations:

1) Gide's *Journals* are presented as an illustration of
his sincereity. But they afford an ultimately distorted
image of their author, for they lack "artificial" retouches.

2) Gide tells us that he has suppressed the pages he regarded as too composed, too "written." By this we understand that the effort of style distorted their spontaneity,
and they are therefore condemned as insincere.

3) And yet a certain lightness with which he assumes a
position—whichever one he takes, and despite his genius
for scruple—on infinitely complex social or theological
questions cannot be explained except by an *artist's* defiance of ideas as such, of methodical analysis, and of all
that may burden the rhythm of thought. To insist, to argue,
to cite sources and facts would still be sincerity, in relation
to the object; but it would spoil the spontaneous impulse
of sentiment, no less than the elegance of style.

All this proceeds from a conception of sincerity which

we might call *descriptive:* it confines itself, voluntarily, to revealing and remarking the most secret fluctuations of the natural individual. It refuses conventional simplifications, the prejudices of morality, its selfish silences, in short, the censures which tend to reduce spontaneous contradictions. It would adopt an attitude of welcoming impartiality toward the individual. "Others form man, I recite him," it seems to say with Montaigne. And yet we sense that it masks a polemical reservation, and also a certain desire for justification; in sum, it insinuates that morality is false, and that our contradictions are legitimate. It also adduces, despite its intention, implicit value judgments, under cover of which new regions of what is human can be expressed.

To this sincerity, which intends to describe without bias and which admits in fact nothing that is not spontaneous, I oppose a sincerity that we may call *constructive.* Everything exists in man, it would say, but not everything is of equal value. And it is not hypocrisy, quite the contrary, to declare its values. Our contradictions are real, our ethical hierarchies no less so; but the latter tend to reduce the former by a series of vital choices in which the being-in-action is expressed, that is, his dominant tendency, the style of his existence. It is in this somewhat broadened sense that we might repeat that *style is the man.* In us, style is the revealing characteristic of an intentional unity, of a resolution as sincere, if not more so, than the plurality of instinctive drives. To establish, by noting them, certain contradictions of mood is sometimes less

to "recite oneself" than to distort oneself. For a micro-
scopic introspection is not without its effect on life; it introduces into the combinations to be studied a quantum
of lucidity which modifies the natural *donnéės*.

Now it is very curious to discover that Gide adopts in
his life—as his *Journals* reveal that life—the first conception of sincerity, whereas his entire work is dominated by
the second.

All of Gide's esthetic—his written style—is organized
around a most classical choice: concision, epitome, sacrifice of the incident to the essential, and of spontaneous
expansion to the pure line of the phrase. It is a discipline
of mind, or better, an ethic of expression; ultimately a
very refined civility or strict austerity of the word. The
Calvinism the Prodigal Son fled from returns in force in
the style of the narrative! Astonishing paradox of a
chastened esthetic, ordering a work whose great message
is that we must free ourselves from rules.

To the fictional interviewer who asks him what ethics
are, Gide answers: a dependency of esthetics. Now, not
only does the example of his life not confirm this sally
but the example of his art tends to reverse it: It is in his
esthetic that his most rigorous ethic takes refuge, and
there prevails to the point where one might say that the
former depends on the latter. This goes as far as casuistry:
Gide's passionate interest in the subtlest details of style is
attested by a hundred pages of the *Journals*. I am not forgetting that he has deleted the pages he regarded as too
"written." But what remains cannot deceive us. One does

not get rid of morality so easily, even when it is disguised as semantic scruple. A stylist has as much difficulty "writing badly," or "not writing," as a Puritan "letting himself go." And if the Puritan is a stylist of morality, Gide remains a Puritan of stlyle.

Perhaps we have come to the principle of the revelatory intimate hierarchy of his *person*. This would be the tension instituted between an esthetic exigency, whose principle is properly "moral," and an ethic, which seeks to be "immoralist." A tension ultimately resolved to the—enigmatic—benefit of morality, that is, of rule and choice.

Rules and choices—to adapt and to create—are the conditions of all culture. Yet I have spoken of Gide's *artist's mistrust* of "ideas." It is here that I feel most distinctly the distance that separates my generation from his.

Our culture is much more philosophical—I simplify—than literary, though not by preference, far from it. We have not been able to choose the problems that beset us, and still less to circumscribe them within a privileged domain: that of letters and their morality, which is esthetics. Such problems sometimes constrain us more than they serve our natural tastes, whence the risk of didacticism, a risk we all run to some degree. In this regard, it seems to me that Gide's lesson, for my generation, is less urgent in the order of ethics than in that of esthetics. It is the master-artisan of the language more than the immoralist who matters to us, and who *interests* us in both senses of the word. Yet I would not exclude a reversal in the generations to come; I foresee the day when our juniors will confront us with the example of the clearsighted adversary of vainglorious orthodoxies which Gide, we need have no doubts, will remain to the end.

—*June, 1939*

# Prototype E. T. L.

Surrounded by extragavant attention, subject to exceptional ordeals, studied down to the smallest detail of his often unpredictable behavior, the prototype may reveal himself as unsuitable for mass production; his interest is not thereby diminished. For he affords a new knowledge of certain *limits* of speed, resistance, or flexibility—what happens when they are reached? How far can they be extended? And at what cost? All this will ultimately serve to help us construct better machines. I propose to regard T. E. Lawrence as the prototype of a race of writers of whom this century furnishes several examples often less pure or less complete.

Lawrence was a writer only by accident, it seems. But this accident created his glory, and alone gives us the possibility and the desire to discuss him. Many others have had similar adventures, but he "knew what he was doing, while the others worked by instinct."[1] *The Seven Pillars of Wisdom* and all his letters bear witness to a deliberate awareness, a will to expression which justifies this essay's point of departure.

## i   The Twentieth-Century Writer-hero

In order to distinguish the *exemplary singularity* of Lawrence's case, we must resort not only to the analysis of the work in itself, but first of all consider the role this work played in the conflict between the author and his age.

[1] *Letters,* p. 412.

The seventeenth-century writer seems to us naturally integrated in the society of his time; the eighteenth-century writer scarcely less so, though he calls into question or jeers excessively—but from *inside,* where he is established—the principles of the existing order (Rousseau, virtually alone, breaks his ties with it). After Napoleon, everything changes. There appears the new race of exiles-at-home—Kierkegaard, Baudelaire, and Nietzsche are typical—men exiled in the negation of an order which surrounds without incorporating them, exiled in nihilism, exiled in transcendence. There is no further common measure between the man who thinks and those who act; thus, there is no further real community. And that is why the twentieth century will see so many nomads and actual expatriots.

Some travel to climates and customs where social isolation, without being surmounted, is at least compensated for by some sense of chosen participation (Rilke across Europe; Gide in Africa; D.H. Lawrence in Italy and Mexico; Bernanos in Majorca and Brazil; Joyce in Trieste, Switzerland, and France; Hemingway in Spain and Africa). Others exile themselves in a rootless career as mariners or diplomats (Joseph Conrad, Claudel, St. John Perse). And many have found themselves exiled by the political party which had confiscated their country (from Silone to Koestler, including Germans, Spaniards, Russians, and Eastern Europeans).

Some, finally, set out in search of a community they could join or create in action, and here alone words may recover a meaning and language an authentic power. But such men think first of action, and in action of self-realization, of measuring the power of a man against the world and the self. Is this, too, a compensation? A lover's quarrel can make a man chaste or on the contrary hurl him into debauchery. And, similarly, the communitarian dispute can provoke an exasperated individualism or, on the contrary, the decision to serve, without many illusions, a cause whose value is less important than the ordeals it imposes.

Here we are close to Lawrence and to a class of writers who will doubtless remain most typical of our century.

They are heroes by something other than by their works: by the action to which those works attest and from which they derive their particular effectiveness. For action serves as a pledge (*gage*) for words, and in this technical sense these men are pledged (*engagé*); they have paid with their person the price of a signification.

That these heroes should be nomads is, then, generally accountable. Most run their risks away from home, secretly irritated as they are to feel alien among their own people. To expatriate oneself becomes a clarification, a spatial translation of the conflict which they observe between their inner demands and the insipidity of the slack life of their cities. (Some have found in the army, and especially in the air services, the means of expatriating themselves without crossing their country's borders. The aviator is always on the point of departure, and thereby separated from everyday existence: "First point: we are not tied to the ground," Lawrence wrote, apropos of the R.A.F.)

They seek their adventures away from home, like conquerors and like revolutionaries. This characteristic deserves special attention. Few are originally partisans, and perhaps several of them were resigned, in their countries, to the existing political status. Byron, in this regard, would be the extreme example, for he died to liberate the Greeks, yet did nothing to gainsay the rights of the Lords or the capitalists in England. Actually, it is a love of the struggle against life, with comrades given by chance, that flings them into enterprises in which the technique of (even pacific) conquest is identified with that of conspiracy. We find them engaged by choice in hazardous conquests, which their governments reluctantly support and sometimes discourage in secret, or in revolutions which others have started and which are no longer at the stage of claims but of shots, requiring less political conviction than boldness or discipline, love of sacrifice or the will to power.

The specific examples of Jünger, Edschmid, Koestler, and Malraux in their first periods; better still, of T. E. Lawrence, Saint-Exupéry, of Richard Hillary; and even of Ernst von Salomon and Ernest Hemingway come to mind in support of these general remarks and afford as many nuances, moreover, as we could wish. However diverse we find them to be by their moral or literary value, by the importance, too, of their historical roles and the sincerity of their convictions, all these men are, or were, individualists in search of a common action, an action performed in foreign parts, and whose ultimate goals mattered less to them than the experience itself, the fact of serving or of testing the limits of man. These *engagé* anarchists can be recognized by a certain sign: Between them and the role they play, often at great danger, there is always a margin of consciousness. And in this margin their written work is produced.

Often the author of a single book, under varying titles, few of them are born writers, in the current sense of the expression, which posits not only talent but a certain facility. This is because they have formed themselves in a world where error involves immediate sanctions, where exactitude is vital, whether in drafting an order or commanding a technical operation. These scruples over subduing the precise meaning to rhythm or the play of syllables can spoil the movement of a text: They do not care. The best of them compensate on a profounder level of linguistic effectiveness: Certain formulas to manipulate minds, and especially to impose a determined angle of vision upon them—which is the whole secret of command —are either known to them or instinctive. It is not only to their reputations as adventurers, revolutionaries, or aviators that the particular prestige of their writings is due but as much to the effectiveness of a syntax which knows how to "take hold" (*saisir,* a favorite expression of Saint-Exupéry's).

Let us repeat that these writings are not, for them, substitutes for a completed action or a temporarily suspended one, but rather attempts to find a meaning for it, and to justify the author for having undertaken it. Yet such testimony is ambiguous; autobiographical by nature, it yields few confidences. These men rarely confess any other ambition than that of a servant of the collective cause, and afford only a simplified and suitably stylized portrait of the individual. Born of the need to explain themselves, their works remain obscure on a decisive point: that of the final goals which the author pursues when he lived what he is telling. We then turn to their posthumous writings, to letters or private journals, and we realize that the problem, far from receiving the looked-for-answer here, appears only the more fundamental: It is to attempt to solve it that the man writes, and that he sometimes returns to action; yet, what he finally leaves us is only a question, the example of a "passion" whose stake is not clear. And, of course, the vicissitudes of such a passion may be quite enough for the interest of the work. They make almost all our fictions pale. They force us to believe that here, at last, a man is speaking to us with the authority of a virile experience carried to extremes, in moral and physical rigor. But yielding to the very need wakened by such an example, we ask: *why* these inhuman ordeals? Neurosis, or a search for "lay" sanctity? By what sovereign goals can we justify them? If we answer that they strip man down to his severest truth, we then ask: What will dress him again in a  truer vocation than the causes he has served and which always turn out to be finally disappointing?

## ii   T.E.L. and St.-Ex

"Ambition is a despicable motive: love of freedom an illusion: patriotism, difficult when those, as Lawrence says, who love England most are often those who love the English least; as for honor, it is easier to die for it than to live for it; and better to die than drive others, by intrigue and cruelty, toward the final disillusion." It is in such terms that the soberest of Lawrence's biographers[2] describes the state of mind of the thirty-year-old hero at the end of his Arabian campaigns, before the greatest failure of his hopes at the Versailles Conference. But how can we help thinking of Saint-Exupéry?

The parallel between these two figures is inevitable. That they were so different in so many respects, so contrasted in their individual qualities, merely emphasizes the interest of a comparison between the two *persons*. Let us first examine the differences, in order to determine more clearly the human formula which, despite everything or almost everything, is common to them.

One is English, the other French, and although both lived their adventures abroad, both are perfect representatives of their nations in what most differentiates them from each other. One is Protestant, the other Catholic, and although both left their faith, they are irrevocably marked by two moralists as extreme in their domains as hostile to one another: the Puritan and the Jesuit. One is an ascetic, the other a *bon vivant*. One is chaste, the other happily repeating that woman is the warrior's rest. One is tormented by scruples in action and full of humor in discussing his written work, the other lustily narrates his adventures and insists on reading to his friends the successive versions of his books in progress. One is reserved to the point of total silence, the other is forever

[2] Charles Edmonds.

seeking a friendly audience. One is tiny and tough, the other big and nervous. It is difficult to imagine two men with more strongly contrasted characters. Everything that in each formed the individual—race, nation, milieu, religion, physical nature, temperament, habits—can be opposed, term for term. But now let us consider their *person,* I mean what they have done with these native *données,* the tensions they have instituted between what they were and what they wanted to be. Let us consider their creation, their action, and their drama. One and the same structures of destiny seems to govern these two lives.

Their vocation is marked from childhood and confirmed during adolescence; by twenty they have set out, one for excavations in those Arab countries he had studied so passionately, the other in the planes he was already trying to operate on the sly at the age of sixteen. These two intellectuals who always remain so curious about the literary avant-garde—one turned toward history and the other toward the sciences, but both inventors of machines—will choose professions in which technique is combined with the art of command and risk with discipline. Their work is performed in teams, with rough and hardened comrades. Much more, this work takes them far from their own nations, to wild regions. Here they are doubly exiled and, by the most curious coincidence, dealing with the same Arabs in the desert. Whether negotiating with them in order to liberate a comrade taken as a hostage, or inciting them to revolt, in both cases it is essential to speak their language, penetrate their ways of thought, assimilate the subtle methods which establish the prestige

of their leaders. From this prolonged commerce and from
the custom of the desert, both will keep the secret of in-
fluencing and manipulating men by means which are not
those of the rule-book and which owe nothing to official
qualifications: a love of authority, not power. (Lawrence,
later, will reproach himself for this, but not St.-Ex.) Both
deride rank, whether it is accorded them or not, and are
perpetually on a footing of insurrection. Their contempt
for the dangerless functions of those from whom they
receive orders gives the measure of their sense of service:
They submit not to the functionary, but to the mysterious
virtue they expect from regulations, even when they are
unjust. Further, their greatest actions are performed despite the jurisdiction of superior powers. Occasionally,
however, this art of persuasion (which they derive in part
from the Arabs) wins them surprising support on the part
of a great leader whom they have been able to beguile
without passing through the channels of service.

Thus, they are formed by their actions, tempered by
dangers and disappointments and by the severely won
successes which their teammates are often the only ones
to know about. And they turn back toward the world of
*the others,* and this is the beginning of disgust.

Objective sign of a profound disjunction: They enter
into conflict with the policy of their nations' governments,
the very ones they have just served, but whose goals or
methods are suddenly revealed to be incompatible with
the spirit in which they have served. A more personal sign:
they confess in their letters the profoundest and best-
motivated doubts as to the value of the action by which

they have made themselves illustrious. (Physical courage they never mention, except with a skepticism quite without coquetry.) Their only explicit desire from this time on is to retire to some house in the country with the book they bear within them, always the same, and which must be a commentary on their action, intended to save that action from historical anecdote in order to extract from it a universal wisdom, and to raise a "lasting" or "intangible" monument to the memory of a collective effort.

They write no more easily one than the other, boasting sometimes, but more frequently complaining, of their excessive exactingness and their infinite reworkings. This is because they refuse the lures of ideology or lyricism, apply themselves to exact descriptions, and generally work within a psychology which confounds classical morality and its nomenclature; yet they seek to be simple and to use only familiar words. . . . It is at this stage that *The Seven Pillars of Wisdom* and *Wind, Sand and Stars* are born. The adventure seems to be consummated. And yet their most typical drama reaches a climax at this very moment, confronted with the temptation of the "normal life" of a writer laden with hero's honors.

Instead of retiring to a house in the country or accepting some public function, they suddenly return to their service. They willingly lose themselves in the ranks, submitting to the most abject disciplines. Both explain this behavior by varying and even contradictory reasons. In both cases, and despite different historical circumstances, it seems difficult to distinguish the true motives among so many excuses that they allege. Is it an escape from their social "character" or a real passion to serve? Or is it merely that they have no choice, and that life among the others, the civilians, has proved to be practically untenable for them? ("Do you understand that I enlisted not to write books but because I was stony broke?" Lawrence wrote in 1923. Hence the money is only a symbol: He could earn it in other ways.)

Naturally their superiors, embarrassed by these cumbrous glories (these "unicorns" as Lawrence said), do their best to discourage them; but they persist, though they are older than their comrades, though they have had "all their limbs broken" (St.-Ex.) during their preceding campaigns, though they are obsessed by their need to write, and though they cannot be unaware that at less anonymous posts they would be more difficult to replace. It is an inextricable tangle of pride and masochism, modest loyalty and wounded self-regard, of sabotage against society and submission to the rules of its game. The same enigmas, moreover, without any better solution, were posed in the past by certain religious vocations, and this analogy does not fail to strike them. Lawrence describes his enlistment in the air force as "the best modern equivalent of entering a monastery in the middle ages." Both are separated from faith and perhaps ultimately from faith in themselves or in the role they may still play among men as they see them. "I have come to the point of constantly wanting the curtain to fall. It is as though I were through now," Lawrence writes a few weeks before his death. (And Saint-Exupéry, in all his last letters, has sentences in the same tone.)

The moment of the forced retreat approaches—the end of his enlistment period for one, of the war for the other— and the fatal accident occurs. Each is killed by the machine which had been the passion of his life.

But their legends prevail against the facts. For a long time, people refuse to believe they are dead; have they not turned up again after so many other dangers? And perhaps they have vanished only to assume other tasks, more secret and more important ones?[3]

## iii   Beyond Catchwords of the Age

I shall now attempt to answer the question from which these pages derive: "What does Lawrence mean to us?"

Dictators are the heroes of the masses, which generate them out of their terror of a freedom without content. There are all kinds of dictators, it is true, but prostitution

[3] Each sentence, each nuance of this parallel could be supported by specific documents and by frequent quotations from the books or letters of the two men. I have been obliged to confine myself to paraphrasing them, the last letters of Saint-Exupéry having not yet been published.

As for *La Citadelle*, it will be noted that it has no equivalent in Lawrence's *oeuvre*. And, of course, nothing prevents us from supposing that Lawrence, had he lived in peace in his cottage, might have been tempted by an analogous work, a lyrical and "literary" transposition of the experiences of a man of action. But we know that Churchill intended him for important military functions, which the war would doubtless have obliged him to accept. On the whole, Saint-Exupéry was more a writer, Lawrence an agent of history.

is common to them all: They lend themselves to the lowest lusts, as, for instance, to the collective narcissism which is nationalist passion. I see their antithesis in the heroes of personal integrity, of whom Lawrence is the prototype.

The dictator is strong only by others' weakness, and his greatness is negative; he is the symbol of the secret resignations we afford him in order to make a crowd. But the strength of a Lawrence has its source only in the demands he imposes upon himself. The dictator is the parasite of public diseases; Lawrence has never asked anything except of himself. His power over others horrifies him, as he confesses on many occasions. He uses it only with repugnance (and suffers remorse over doing so long afterward), when the necessities of action oblige him to do so, as in his Arabian campaign; and he cannot keep from denouncing this use, even when it is legal, as an abuse. To force others will always be a rape, and if he condemns this rape, it is because he seeks to be whole, at the cost of a sacrifice of which he remains the master. This is his realist heroism: If someone must pay, let it be himself at the expense of his own individual and for the education of his own person. He outstrips all the others in this direction. And he has no equal in the demands he makes on himself, in his contempt for fraud, in his fruitful sense of scruple, except in Kafka, that other prototype.

This is precisely what is exemplary about Lawrence: He has subjected the condition of modern man to the severest tests in various realms, himself bearing the brunt of the experiment and refusing all the evasions furnished by political causes, religious romanticism, and catchwords such as Revolt and Conformism, Freedom, Violence, Anxiety—and the most ambigious of all—Revolution. It is as if he had made upon himself a study of the resistance of human substance and morale under the conditions in which our world finds itself. And here is the result of this study, the best description I can imagine of modern reality as such. Lawrence is in an R.A.F. camp when he writes this letter to Lionel Curtis on May 30, 1923.

And then there is the absence of responsibility: I am accountable here only for the cleanness of my skin, of my clothes, and for a certain precision in physical exercise. Since I've been here, I haven't had a single choice to make: everything is prescribed—with the exception of that agonizing possibility of choosing to leave, should my desire to remain collapse. Aside from that, this is complete determinism—and perhaps complete determinism contains the perfect peace I have sighed after so long. I have tried free will, and rejected it; I have rejected authority (not obedience, for my present effort is an attempt to find equality in subordination alone. It is the exercise of authority that disgusts me); I have rejected action; and intellectual life; and the receptive life of the senses; and competition. So many failures, and my reason tells me that obedience will fail too, since the roots of the common failure must be in me—and yet, despite reason, I am trying it.

Twelve years later, and shortly before his death, he draws from his "tries" the following conclusions: The Near East Statute (which was in part his work in 1921) counts for more than his campaigns in his eyes, but less than his activity in the R.A.F., "for the conquest of the air seems to me to be the only major task of our generation; and I am convinced that progress, today, is not the result of isolated genius, but of the common effort. For me, it is the host of uncouth lorry-drivers covering all the roads of England every night that makes our mechanical age." And it is also the simple mechanics of the R.A.F., not the great aces. "That is why I have remained in the ranks, and I have served my best . . ."

Even the idea of creating something "intangible," which had sustained him in his artist's effort when he was writing *The Seven Pillars of Wisdom,* he denies, for "all creation is tangible. And what I was attempting, I think, was to set a superstructure of ideas on all that I was doing. Well, in that I have failed. So I have taken a different tack . . . I have enlisted in the R.A.F. to put myself at the service of a mechanical enterprise, not as a leader, but as a cog in in the machine. The key-word, I think, is machine . . . I leave others the job of deciding if I have chosen well or badly: one of the advantages of being a part of the machine is that it teaches you that you have no importance."

Such texts can serve as landmarks for those among us who, lacking an acceptable order, try to find an equilibrium in chaos. Landmarks, but not a philosophy. For Lawrence, like several of his race, locates himself in our problems only in a fragmentary manner, on occasions so concrete that the technique he has mastered from experience, the pledge of his honesty, becomes an alibi as well.

From the point of view of our political disputes, to limit ourselves to a burning issue, what may we infer

from his example? The quotations I have just given seem
to indicate that Lawrence would have been quite capable
of justifying, quite attractively, Stalinism and the totalitarian movements in general. Yet he was their adversary,
and he would have fought against them. Must we accuse
him of inconsistency? The problem is somewhat different.
Without any doubt, the *morality* he professes, at the end of
his twelve-year experiment in the air force, is a collectivist
morality (the common effort which achieves progress
being only a cog in the machine, learning to regard oneself
as nothing, finding peace in complete determinism, and
even the cult of the machine!). But, on the other hand,
his aversion to ideology, his rejection of imperialism in all
its forms, particularly moral, his distaste for the necessity
of imposing his power and applying authority—everything opposes him to dictatorship and to collectivist
politics. What remains for such a man to do? I quote him
again: "The ideals of a policy are the kind of things that
work on your feelings: their translation into terms of compromise with the social structure resulting from them is a
secondary matter. I have met no one more honest and devoted than our statesmen, but I would rather be a crossing-
sweeper. A decent nihilism is what I hope for, in general.
I think that a well-constituted nation like ours can allow
itself 1 per cent of monists or nihilists. That leaves room
enough for me. The trouble with Communism is that it
accepts too much of today's furniture. I hate furniture."

Let us not see this as an evasion of the great political
choice of the century: democracy or totalitarianism. These
little sentences of cynical humor, though dashed off in a

hasty letter, express a mature attitude. It is the morality of Kafka's *Castle,* the line of retreat (before metaphysical problems) of a man whose "sorties" have failed and for whom there is no longer any solution but to assure himself a small place in the city, a useful role in this world which he judges quite absurd—by excess of ethical consciousness —but which must still be accepted, when one has not known (or when one refuses) the transcendence which alone can transform it.

An attitude exemplary by its honesty. If we needed the evidence, at the point we have reached, of what a man can do without faith, Lawrence has presented it with great courage, and above all without the least concern for being an example, for instructing, whence his sincerity, through so many disguises. One cannot help loving him. But there is no question of following him. However "decent," nihilism is a poor defense against the monsters of our times. Indeed, objectively, nihilism is their precursor. The false totalitarian faiths have no serious enemy except faith.

Yet to those who say that Lawrence is disappointing because he left no "message," I should answer that he teaches us at least not to expect one from men. We ask too much of writers. On the whole, we expect them to replace religion. The most honest, if he is without faith, admits he has nothing to reveal, but by doing so he describes better the true state of man. Nothing survives the test that has not begun here.

# Four

# A Disease

**of the Person**

# German Romanticism

## i Mysticism and the Dream

The lucid consciousness is the first spiritual conquest of men afflicted by the mystery of an hostile and changing nature. The speech of reason that distinguishes, arrests, and identifies matter appears as a deliverance, a victory over panic chaos. But this victory, when it is too complete, leaves man with a sense of frustration and unspeakable impoverishment. The rational world is reassuring, but many questions in it remain unanswered and many ancestral hungers unsatisfied. So that a new anguish gradually appears, an attraction, comparable to vertigo, toward those obscure regions of being which common sense and philosophy claimed to banish from humanity. And while, in his terror, primitive man had turned toward liberating reason, at the end of the periods impoverished in mystery, the skeptic passionately turns to the "night side" of his nature. Thus German Romanticism was born after the Enlightenment. Thus our elementary mystical thirsts reappear after a century of positivist science.

Is it true that night and dreams have nothing to reveal that matters by day? Is it true that passion, anguish, and madness are less real than our tyrannical wisdom? *"Songe est mesonge"*—dream is falsehood, reason has decreed. But it leaves our hunger unsatiated. The dream, on the contrary, offers us Edens and terrors of a seductive intensity. Is it the sign or the entrance of a higher truth?

This is the question the first German Romantics asked. "They all admit," Albert Béguin writes,[1] "that the obscure life is in constant communication with another vaster reality, anterior and superior to individual life." But what is reality? Our deepest nature or divinity? "The further we withdraw into ourselves, turning away from appearances, the further we penetrate into the nature of the things that are outside us," asserts Ignaz Troxler, one of the theoreticians of Romanticism. But again, is it truly a question of the things that are outside of us or else only of the things which, within us, had remained secret for the consciousness? Tieck puts the question quite clearly: "We must know to what point our dreams belong to us." When we dream, "is it we who play tricks on ourselves, or does a man from on high shuffle the cards?" E.T.A. Hoffmann already suggests the answer: "And what if a spiritual principle alien to ourselves were the motive of these sudden eruptions of unknown images which are flung across our ideas so abruptly and so startlingly?" From this to supposing that the dream is a "vestige of the divine" is only the distance of a qualm of orthodoxy, a final scruple to identify man and God. Troxler skillfully sketches the difficulty and the choice: For him, the dream is "sometime an echo of the supra-terrestrial in the terrestrial, sometimes a reflection of the terrestrial in the supra-terrestrial"; or again, "What dreams in us is the Spirit at the moment of its descent into matter," but it is also "Matter at the moment of its ascent to spirit."

[1] In a splendid book, *L'Ame romantique et le rêve,* from which I draw most of the texts quoted in this essay.

Here is the profound ambiguity from which Romanticism is born and on which it lives! To believe that the dream reveals nothing but *our* secrets would be to fall into Freudianism. To believe that it *also* reveals a higher world is to take the way of the mystics. If most of the Romantics have not chosen very distinctly—a vital ruse for poets—everything suggests that they are closer to the mystics than to the psychoanalysts. When they ask if the dream is knowledge or illusion, and if it is "the Other" or the obscure self that one encounters in the depths of the unconscious, they are formulating the crucial problem raised for all mystics. It is also the crucial problem for any definition of the person. For we are constantly tempted to assimilate the deepest Self and its secret impulses to the Word which comes from Elsewhere, and which alone is true vocation. To a philosopher of the person, it will therefore be of the greatest importance to express the parallel between Mysticism and Romanticism.

First of all, there is the same attention paid to *signs,* to intuitions, to apparently chance encounters, but which the predisposed soul interprets at once as *messages.* This supposes a passionate condition, a certain temperature where all things become translucid, perhaps, too, a long-disappointed nostalgia that greedily seizes on the most furtive promises of happiness, of liberation, of adventure! All Romantic poetry, like Surrealist poetry, is on the alert for the "meaningful surprises" of which the mystics also speak.

Another rather striking analogy is the role of *rhetoric* in the poets of the dream and the mystics. The philosopher

G. von Schubert, as later the poet Jean Paul, insist on a fact which Freud will be the first to give its full value: that the mind abandoned to the dream ordinarily expresses itself in a metaphorical and regular language, as if it were subject, in this realm, to laws more precise and constant than those which govern the waking state. Further, we know that Hindu, Moslem, or Christian mystics have in every period reinvented the same figures of speech to translate the ineffable they experienced.[2]

And this brings us to the central problem: that of *the expression of an unutterable.* Here we must go beyond the circumscribed domain of the dream. The Romantics, moreover, have advanced much farther in their exploration of the unconscious. For them, the dream is only the "door" opening onto the ineffable world, which is strictly the domain of the mystics.

All mystical or Romantic experience presupposes the existence of a *center* or of a divine *substratum* of the soul (Jakob Böhme's *Ungrund*), of which one can say nothing and which is nevertheless the source of all one says. It is the Ineffable, the Unutterable, the Kingdom of absolute Silence; and yet—this is the paradox—we find that the great mystics, and after them the great Romantics, spend their lives talking about it, writing about it, trying to situate

[2] To me, the Freudian error seems to be to individualize the meaning of these symbols and to derive from them a purely sexual key to dreams. C. G. Jung is doubtless closer to reality when he discovers in the figures of our dreams the fundamental religious symbols of the remotest epochs and the most various peoples.

it by figures which, being never adequate, must be inexhaustibly multiplied. We might say, without the slightest irreverence, no one is more verbose than a mystic, if it is not a German Romantic. For both seek to communicate by writing what they unceasingly define as the Unutterable. Thus the complaint will be the same, whether we are dealing with a Theresa of Avila or simply a Ludwig Tieck. Give me "new words" to express the inexpressible, the Saint says; and the poet: "But where *find words* to depict, however weakly, the marvel of the vision that appeared to me, and which, transforming my soul, led me into an invisible, divine reality of an *ineffable* splendor. An *unutterable* delight filled my whole being . . ."

Perhaps here we touch on the mystery itself, the inexhaustible source, the original and fascinating wellspring of language, of all literary expression. "Where find the words?" they groan. The complaint is sincere and tragic, but how many words it will oblige them to accumulate in order to say that nothing can be said.

And yet, Romantics and mystics are convinced that despite their impotence to translate the unconscious or the unutterable, they have heard *something*. "I think I have made an important discovery," Ritter writes, "that of a *passive consciousness of the Involuntary*." And on this foundation the second generation of Romanticism will formulate its famous theory of Inspiration—so vulgarized today that we forget its mystical origin. "The poet and the dreamer are *passive*, they listen to the language of a voice that is within them and yet alien, that rises deep in themselves without their being able to do anything other than greet it as the echo of a divine discourse."[3]

Then doubt is no longer permitted; the purely formal analogy which we hitherto described becomes a profound identity. The intervention of the category of "passivity" makes us realize the nature of the Silence and of the Unutterable, which mystics and Romantics described: It is the negation and death of the world of forms and of human language, the negation and death of variety, of the distinct and functioning self. It is the spiritual night described by John of the Cross, and of which the night of dreams celebrated by the poets was only the symbol and physical sign.[4] It is the "kingdom of Being which is identified with the kingdom of Nothingness, eternity conquered at last and whose plenitude can be humanly expressed only by the image of the Absence of every creature, every form." For we perceive and express only the various and the distinct, what has *taken shape,* what our consciousness has *separated* from the All. And that is what constitutes our everyday reality. To rejoin the All and the One, we must lose the various, lose the real, lose ourselves, in order to be mingled with that Unutterable which remains, in the eyes of the Flesh, pure Nothingness.

Thus the goal of the Romantic search, through the images of the dream, is identified with the goal of every mystical experience; it is "the pure ineffable presence,"

[3] Albert Béguin, *op. cit.*
[4] Indeed, for the Romantics, "sleep is a prefiguration of death," and it is in death alone that we can join the Other, the Unutterable.

"contemplation without object." Thus we are justified in following Albert Béguin to this conclusion: "the greatness of Romanticism will remain to have recognized and affirmed the profound resemblance of poetic states and revelations of a religious order, to have put faith in the irrational powers and to have dedicated themselves body and soul to the great nostalgia of the being in exile."

## ii   The Being in Exile

This sense of exile, which we find at the origin of the most diverse mystical experiences—what is its source, in what memory of a happy and lost homeland? It is easy to reply by instancing our double nature, corporeal and spiritual. But how turn from so general an observation to the elucidation of this most singular fact in the life of the human mind, which is the entry into the *via mystica?*

If it is permitted—as we concede a little too easily in our times—to derive from the study of diseases a new view as to man's structures, perhaps we can seek in the biography of the Romantics some illumination about the mystics proper, at least as to the *human* causes of the sense of of exile in which their passion is wakened. Let us take the example of Karl Philipp Moritz; he offers beyond any other the advantages of a strangely disinterested self-elucidation.

Born in a quietist and pietist milieu, in the middle of the rationalist eighteenth century, Moritz was one of the very first to turn to the study of dreams. He found himself

predisposed to do so by the habit of seaching his consciousness deeply, as the disciples of Mme. Guyon practiced it
around him.[5] Not content with publishing a journal entirely devoted to the analysis of dreams, Moritz wrote two
autobiographical novels which permit us to penetrate the
intimacy of a premystical experience. (Or should we say,
of a mystical experience without grace, reduced to its
purely human aspects?)

The point of departure seems to be a *wound* he received
from life, a shock which left him gaping over the irremediable contradiction between harsh reality and the profound
desires of the self. A wound so cruel and deep that his
consciousness avoided the memory of it (or repressed it,
as Freud will say), so that the secret cause of his pain
comes to be identified with the mere fact of being alive.
Whence the idea that he must *expiate the sin which he has
committed by merely being alive.* A mystical philosopher
like Ignaz Troxler will not hestitate to extend the process
to include the whole universe assailed by original sin:
"From whatever angle one chooses to examine him, man
finds in himself a wound which lacerates all that lives in
himself, and that perhaps produced his very life." Not
without lucidity, Moritz has been able to depict the state
of consciousness which results from this obscure lacera-
tion: "It was as if the weight of his existence had crushed
him. That he must, day after day, get up with himself, go
to bed with himself, drag about with him, at every step,

---

[5] We cannot overemphasize the importance of quietism for the
formation of modern psychology, and in particular for the
psychology of the unconscious.

*his detested self* . . . that he must henceforth inexorably be himself . . . this idea gradually plunged him into a despair which led him to the river bank . . ." Let us note: this *detested self* is the fatality of the individual, carnal, created being, linked to all creation. It is by and through this individual that consciousness can perceive external reality; like this individual then, reality will appear to be wounded and suffering. To hate oneself comes down to hating the world. The incapacity to accept the real world is the sign of an incapacity to accept oneself—on account of this wound which one must forget *if one does not manage to expiate it.* And, in fact, by means of this forgetting, this refusal, the self gradually loses its reality; whence the feeling, so frequent among most of the Romantics, of being unsure of their own identity and of having to seek it precisely in the past. Thus Moritz describes the hero of one of his novels: "It seemed to him that he had entirely escaped himself and that he must first of all seek himself out in the series of his recollections. He felt that existence had no firm support save in the uninterrupted chain of memories."[6] But, as Albert Béguin points out, Moritz at this point "stops short, incapable once again of grasping the saving thought." This is because there is a forbidden memory, one too painful to be experienced again. The diseased self fails to apprehend itself in memory, because the cause of its disease is precisely what it cannot recall to mind, that wound which is at the origin of its divided consciousness.

Then how break the circle, how be cured? How recu-

[6] This is Proust's *A la Recherche du temps perdu.*

perate the whole life in its blessed unity? It is no longer possible here on earth, in the prison of the guilty and suffering self. One must seek beyond. And we have seen that the dream, or the descent into the depths of the unconscious, represents for the Romantics the ways of a return to the lost world, to the "real life" which is "elsewhere," as Rimbaud says. A life of infinite expansion in the universe or in the divinity, a life of recovered innocence, for the self, which here loses itself, also loses the sense of its guilt.

But in still another, and more precise, manner, the dream or the *via mystica* are means of recuperating the lost world. What we must emphasize here is that the tendency to pantheist or mystical dilation of being almost always assumes the form of a *death wish*. Sleep prefigures death for the Romantic poet, and a gradual death to oneself is the ambition of all true mystics. But why does one seek to die? The biographies of most of the Romantics furnish the same answer here. In effect, the wound from which they suffer is almost always symbolized by the loss of a loved being. To pass into the other world is to recover dead beloved! "The typical experience, which is that of Jean Paul upon the death of his friends, of Novalis losing Sophie von Kuhn, of Guérin meditating on the death of Marie, or of Nerval pursuing the image of Aurélia, has been Anton Reiser's (Moritz's hero) from childhood, when he questions himself as to what has become of his little sister: *the desire to find death, to communicate with another universe,* makes him despise this life, feel its limits, put all his hope in an existence beyond the grave."[7]

[7] Albert Béguin, *op. cit.*

The dream or the *via mystica* will be this existence beyond the grave, experienced here on earth in an unutterable way. And perhaps one might say that the general mystical experience becomes strictly Christian only in the case where the beloved being, on whose death one meditates, is the person of the crucified Christ—or is indistinguishably merged with it. The Romantics did not go this far on the way of sublimation, except perhaps Jean Paul and Novalis. They did not manage to rediscover, in their Beyond, a presence which pardons, which cures, and which then affords them the strength to accept their guilty self and the real world. The "contemplation without object" to which they attain at very rare moments is then no more than a means of enjoying a "voluptuous sensation," as Moritz says, of their own dissolution; an indirect way of reviving their wound, or rather the very impetus which the wound has broken, but without admitting it to themselves and without being able to acknowledge or express it. . . . This is the fundamental movement of all *passion,* the movement of a love which prefers nothingness to life's limitations, the death-welcoming joy of Tristan and Isolde. . . .

## iii   Mysticism and the Person

The example of the German Romantics illustrates a profound and constant relationship in man, one which exists between the recourse to the Unutterable and the evasion of the personal self.

To take refuge in the Unutterable is to maintain an ambiguity which, there is reason to fear, is a selfish one.

On the contrary, *to express oneself is always to confess oneself,* is to make oneself responsible for one's thought and actions. Whence their evasion into a world of which nothing can be said. Whence, too, the need they feel to assert superabundantly that nothing can be said of it except by illusions, metaphors, "inspired" poems. On this level, mysticism produces the most moving literature. But we must also acknowledge that it also reveals a disease of the person.

The paradox of the expression of an Unutterable is so essential to Romanticism that it explains, beyond any doubt, the incapacity of most of Goethe's young contemporaries to produce finished works. In fact, the impulse of these poets is the contrary of the creator's. To create is to give form, and they would deny forms; it is to limit, and they aspire to infinite expansion; it is to define by act and speech, and they seek passive silence. Thus they have generally left only fragments, allusions, fugitive flashes, or "illuminations," like the memories of a fading dream. *That thing* which they desire to speak of, that Unutterable or that wordless discourse heard in the night of passivity— how could they bring it into the light without betraying it and themselves? Thus their work is in the image of the vital contradiction from which they suffered and from which was born their anguished desire to lose their personal self. But the personal self is the creative shadow of the natural individual. Let us return one last time to our definitions.

The person in us is the spiritual being, responsible for a vocation and finding his unity in it despite contradictions from which the *individual,* that is, the natural being, may suffer. The individual is entirely determined by species, milieu, history, the qualities he has inherited and the wounds he has suffered. He is imprisoned in these *données,* and it is in vain that he seeks to escape them by sublimations; in the depths of the Night and the Unconscious, it is still himself that he will find under unrecognizeable aspects and which he will be tempted to believe divine. And it is proper that the first touch of the Spirit should make the self sensitive to its limitations and inspire it with a nostalgia to transcend them. But only a *vocation* will give the self strength to do so. If the self receives and consciously accepts its vocation, it will be introduced to an entirely new freedom. From this moment, it undergoes in *appearances* an evolution quite similar to that of those pseudo- or pre-mystics who were the poets of the dream; dedicated to something that transcends it, the self surrenders to a reality which often does not take account of our reasons, undertakes a kind of ascesis which frees it from the natural servitudes. But this ascesis does conclude in the negation of the real. It transforms and reorients the forces of the individual, rather than seeking to destroy them. It engages in the active world, whereas the Romantic sought to evade it. It makes us, finally, responsible to our neighbor, and that is how we may recognize the legitimacy of a vocation. Theresa of Avila was willing to accept only the revelations which led her to some practical action in daily life. Thus the "personalist ascesis" is radically distinguished from the Romantics' dissolution of the self. It is an activity, and begins only beyond the death to oneself, that is, beyond the renunciation of the self tormented by its egoism. It does not take death as a goal, but life, and life on earth. It accepts the self and all its servitudes by virtue of its vocation, that is, by virtue of an appeal from elsewhere but which concerns this life. Only such a vocation can give the courage to confess oneself in utter lucidity, to express oneself without reticence and to assume one's guilty self, because henceforth that is not what counts but the work to be done and He who commands it.

Then the guilty and loathed self no longer seeks a vain evasion into the Unutterable and the Unconscious. It dares speak at last and bear witness in the name of a Truth which transcends it. And here we return to the evangelical teaching; it is no unutterable ecstasies that are promised to the true believers but on the contrary they are asked to act and to announce their faith. "For thou shalt be his witness unto all men of what thou hast seen and heard."

## iv   Collective Repercussions of Anti-personalist Romanticism

Kierkegaard criticized his age in the name of the Solitary's faith, fundamental reality of all existence in the world. But if faith is the Solitary's health, it is also what brings him into communion with his neighbor before God. If the health of faith establishes the true person, it must also establish the true community. And, inversely, every disease of the person must affect the collectivity.

Thus, to describe a mass phenomenon in terms of an etiology of the person would be to furnish the necessary counterpart of the Kierkegaardian analyses. Let us, then, sketch a description of the National-Socialist phenomenon, starting from the categories we have just set up, which refer to the romantico-mystic disease of the person.

The Hitler movement, in its essence, seems to me a kind of political Romanticism. And I am not saying that the writings of a Novalis or a Jean Paul are at its source—that would be absurd and insulting for these poets. But I am saying that we can find, at the lower and collective level which is that of the Nazi psychology, certain processes quite analogous to those we have described. It is not a question of the reviviscences—vulgar, simplistic, cheap— of certain attitudes of man confronting his destiny and his person.

National-Socialism appears to be a kind of defense reaction to the collective humiliation inflicted upon the Germans by Versailles, by defeat, by public misery. That is the wound, the disappointment no longer experienced by an individual but by a whole nation in its relations with the real world. Whence the sentiment of a *guilt* inacceptable and inadmissible (on account of national pride). It is the world which must be wrongly constituted, for we are persecuted by it; we who are nonetheless the sons of the virtuous Teutons! And from this feeling of guilt, strongly repressed and noisily denied (all Hitler's speeches proclaim from the start that the Germans have not lost the war), must result a feeling of national lack of confidence. The true Germany cannot be the one which has suffered the "wound." So it must be sought elsewhere: in a dream of power and liberation in the future, that *ersatz* beyond. Let us deny, then, this reality which oppresses us so meticulously, all these articles in the treaty which accuse us, all these rules of the political game invented by rationalists; what we want is a new passion!

And just as the Romantic forgot his loathed self by sinking into the pomps of his dream, the average German will forget his miseries and the humiliations of his country by losing himself in the collective soul, the hypnosis of celebrations organized by the Führer to the slow and spell-binding rhythm of torchlight parades lasting hours at a time. He is told that he does not count as a conscious individual; he is told that his real life is in the hands of the Party, an anonymous and obscure demiurge from which he can only receive orders without trying to understand them; he is to be "passive." Hence he is liberated from the terrible responsibility of his consciousness and his doubts. The collective discipline plays the role of an ascesis. The very renunciations it imposes become the proofs of its transcendent truth. And this is how the German masses, imitating the Romantic evolution on the lowest level, hope to recover their lost unity in a supra-personal world where the hostile limits fade away, where passion can flourish, where intensity of emotion replaces the paltry truth of jurists. And this clarifies many things that at first glance seem unconnected: the suppression of Roman law, the contempt for frontiers and obligations, the cult of the dead re-established, the dream of infinite expansion, but also the love of war (prefiguration of death, always dreamed of by the great men of passion), and the desire to imprison oneself in an impenetrable, unutterable, incommunicable reality which has no "reasons" to offer, a material and moral *autarchy*.

We cannot overemphasize to what degree this Romantic

pseudo-mysticism determined the Führer's entire action and his hypnotic power over the masses. The appearances of *Realpolitik,* maintained by the cynical and the skillful, have dissimulated only very imperfectly the true well-springs of the Hitler regime. We are no longer in the presence of Bismarck, but of a people bewitched by its dream, a people who renounced reason, gave over justifying itself in the world's eyes because it found in its passion a kind of exalting innocence, an occasion for sacrificing its guilty and loathed self to something truer than life, and which was its millennial mission. "In Germany," Goebbels proclaimed, "we do not impose upon the people various opinions among which it must choose: the people does not like to choose, it likes to be offered a fair opinion. . . . Moreover our politics is a politics of artists. The Führer is an artist of politics. Other statesmen are only laborers. The Führer's State is the product of an imagination of genius."[8]

A politics of "artists," a politics of collective Romanticism, *but for the use of Philistines*—that is the nightmare the sleepwalking Third Reich will have dreamed. A religious disease more than a political one, whose causes must be sought in the most secret depths of the German consciousness, in the drama where the fate of each person is played out. Yes, whether it is a question of the solitary man or of the masses, this drama will always be the same; it is the confrontation of a religion of the collective Unconscious by a faith that seeks to bear witness by the Word and the *personal* act.

*—July, 1939*

[8] Speech of June 18, 1939, in Danzig.